IF I WERE
SEVENTEEN AGAIN
And Other Essays

Jesse Stuart

ARCHER EDITIONS PRESS

IF I WERE SEVENTEEN AGAIN
AND OTHER ESSAYS

First Edition

Design by Wanda Hicks

Library of Congress Cataloging in Publication Data
Stuart, Jesse, 1907–
    If I were seventeen again, and other essays.
    I. Title.
PS3537.T9251613   814'.5'2   79-25079
ISBN 0-89097-016-5

INTRODUCTION

From the day I entered what was to me my first big world of books and learning, I was fascinated by the essay, a literary category exercised greatly by practically all of the English writers from the Elizabethan Period, through the Victorian Period and until September 1922. Also, I learned there were prominent American essayists beginning with our infant American Literature which included such greats as Henry David Thoreau and Ralph Waldo Emerson. Emerson became a favorite of mine in the essay as Robert Burns became a favorite in poetry.

I found these essays and biographical sketches of their authors in the Greenup High School Library. Greenup High School barely exceeded one hundred pupils and the Library was very small. But one good book can influence a youth as I was one who was influenced by a few good books in this little Library.

Before entering Greenup High School I had gone to Plum Grove, a one-room rural school for twenty-two months, which certainly didn't have a library and where one teacher taught all grades from first to eighth, fifty-six classes in six hours. I am one who can honestly say the American youth of today have great educational opportunities, even if their schools are "poor" as so many critics say. We have come a long way, education-wise, in my day and time in this country. I think today education and opportunities are handed to the American youth on a platter. He doesn't have to fight to get an education.

In little Greenup High School, I read my first novel, *Silas Mariner*. I read poetry, short stories and essays. English Literature was predominant over American Literature. The "Concord Group" was predominant in our American Literature. For me, Ralph Waldo Emerson was "tops" of a group who were all from excellent to good. So it was here I read my first essays. And I liked the essay. I read everyone I could lay my hands on in our limited library. I thought Charles and Mary Lamb were great.

I never knew in those youthful days that someday I would be writing essays. I didn't know then that editors in the future would be accepting one of my articles for a short story or one of my intended article-short stories for an essay. But this is the way it has been, times too numerous to mention. Over the years, from time to time, I've constantly had accepted and published items that could not be categorized as article or short story. They could be on the border but really not one of them.

Many of my essays were written for speeches. They were later published as essays. "What America Means To Me," was written after one of my prolonged travels. I do this often for I don't believe anybody knows America until he has seen other countries to which he can compare his native land. I've travelled in ninety countries. I can well remember after one of these prolonged travels, after my wife and I returned, we were invited by friends to come and see a football game at Ohio University (a favorite school of mine). As much as I like football (played semi-pro football), in that heated contest, I sat watching the American flag the entire game. I thought what it meant to all of us. I had thoughts there of writing an essay on the American flag which I never did. I let this idea slip. I should have been writing it there instead of pretending to watch the game.

Some of my essays are very much like the early English essays where nature and the small things around the writer, such as "The Little Pencil Reminder on My Desk," play a part. Essay subjects can be very simple ones, yet a readable and stirring piece can be extracted. Back somewhere in my life, I read essays on A Ball of Twine, A Ball of Mud and Polish the Heels of Your Shoes. I have written about simple things and feelings. It will please me if my readers like them. If they don't I'm sorry that they have wasted their good time, time that will not come again.

Jesse Stuart

Jesse Stuart

CONTENTS

Jesse Stuart with dog

WHAT AMERICA MEANS TO ME

Today in Milwaukee I spoke to approximately 14,400 educators from the State of Wisconsin. It was my first time ever to speak to so many people assembled under one roof. This audience was so large it scared me. It was hard for me to realize that so many people were listening to me.

After my talk, teachers came up and brought my books for me to sign. It was a great meeting for me. I had never dreamed in my youth of addressing an audience of this size. And I had never dreamed when I wrote poems on poplar leaves and scraps of paper I picked up along the road, that more than 1000 people at Baylor University, in Waco, Texas, would pay to hear me read them. At the same university the next morning I signed 176 books. When the books ran out I autographed slips of paper for students and others.

I had never dreamed, either, that I would travel in 39 states in one year, give 76 talks, speak to more than 100,000 people of teacher groups, colleges, universities, and civic organizations . . . I am not bragging when I mention these things. I feel humble. It is hard to believe it happened to me. And my feeling is that my name had a better chance of becoming known in my native country than it would have had in any part of the world where I have been.

I have traveled in 29 foreign countries and 44 states in the United States and approximately half the provinces of Canada. So, when I sign my name and when people say kind words for some of the things I have written, my mind flashes back to another day and time. It goes back to the little world I knew. And that was the one-room shack in Greenup County, Kentucky, where I was born on a high ridge overlooking the waters of W-Hollow on one side, Shacklerun waters and the Plum Grove hills on the other.

My father, who could not read and write his name at that time, was a coal miner. He dug coal with a pick from low and dangerous mines, where three men lost their lives. Because of the brittle roof, the mines have since been closed. My mother caught rain water in a barrel at the corner of the shack to use for washing our clothes, since the water up where we were on the high hill was sulphur water. She carried water in a lard can from a neighbor's well for drinking and cooking. My mother, in those days, was young and strong. She carried a lard can of water on one hip, carried me on the other because I couldn't climb the hill fast enough, and my oldest sister, Sophia, ran along behind her to keep up.

We had only one book in our shack. That was the Bible. We kept it out on a little table for everyone to see. And above the Bible, with the trigger guard hanging over one spike nail that was driven into a joist, and the end of the long barrel resting on another spike nail, was our shotgun, which my father kept hanging ready to protect his family. Also, to shoot owls when they menaced our white chickens that roosted on the leafless branches of the winter trees. Also, to shoot a fox when he came for a pig or chicken. On a barren puncheon floor, two beds, a cookstove, standtable, and mirror comprised all our worldly possessions. We didn't own the one-room shack. We rented it.

My mother was the educated one in our family. She had finished the second grade and she wrote the letters we had to write, read the few we received. When my father left the coal mine, he moved down into W-Hollow, rented a little farm, where the log shack, which stands today, had ample room for his family. We had too much room—three rooms. He bought a mule and plow and one cow. And he bought young oxen, broke them to the yoke, and plowed the rooty hillsides with them.

And it was my father who preached education for his family. He wanted one of his children to be a schoolteacher, which he thought (and I am inclined to agree after the years have passed) was the greatest profession in the world. School-teaching was the only profession of man that my father ever looked up to. And it was at Plum Grove, a one-room rural school high on a hilltop, that I learned to write. I was so elated to put something down on paper that stood for a real something that I ran home and said to my father, "Pa, I can do something you can't do." He said, "What's that?" I said, "Write my name."

My father was embarrassed. He got my

3

mother to teach him a memorized signature which only the banker in his home town knows today. When my first teacher, Calvin Clarke, who taught me to read and write, told my father that my sister and I were "bright pupils" who ought to stand at the head of our classes, my father was pleased. Calvin Clarke was 18 years old, weighed 110 pounds, taught 56 classes in 6 hours. The Plum Grove attendance ranged from 50 to 70 pupils. Many of his pupils were older than he. They were in their twenties. But to me this school was the greatest place on earth. It wasn't work for me, it was a place of recreation. My schoolbooks were fabulous things in this early dawn of exciting life. And my teacher, Mr. Clarke, a high-school graduate, had all the knowledge in the world, I thought.

My father moved from farm to farm. Always to better his position. There were 10 houses in W-Hollow and we lived in 8 of them. The first house he rented we paid $6 a month cash rent, plus one-third grain rent from our crops. And since we didn't have any fences on this farm, we had to rent pasture for our oxen, mule, and cow. We paid three different kinds of rent.

Since we sold sweet potatoes at 25 cents a bushel, strawberries at 5 cents a quart, tobacco at 3 and 4 cents a pound, eggs at 8 and 9 cents a dozen, I was forced by these circumstances to quit school. I worked by the day for 25 cents. Worked from 10 to 14 hours. My father and his horse worked for $1.50 per day. My mother got 25 cents per day for housework.

My early schooling was limited. I had to leave Plum Grove. But I was schooled in a different way. All the farms I worked on in Kentucky were beautiful in the spring months. I saw nature come to life from winter's sleeping. I learned many things on the land. Learned that the terrapins and turtles laid eggs in the sand and let the warm sun hatch their young. Learned that the cowbird laid eggs in other birds' nests and let them hatch and raise their young. Learned that black snakes laid eggs in the rich, warm loam and the sun hatched their young, while the poisonous copperhead didn't lay eggs.

I learned where all the wild berries grew, learned the names of all the trees and the wild flowers and vines. All the life about me was a great school and while I worked for 25 cents a day I learned. Learned something from the stories told by older men who were working with me.

Finally, my father bought 50 acres of land in the head of W-Hollow for $300. That was a big price for us to pay and we didn't have the money, but my father borrowed it. It was a tract of land, the only one in Greenup County, that didn't have a legal road to it. When we walked to it, in any direction, we had to get permission from land-owners whose farms surrounded ours. We couldn't haul anything to our farm, for there wasn't a wagon road leading to it.

My father was so excited about buying 50 acres of land and becoming a landowner that the day he got the deed he changed from chewing home-grown Burley tobacco and smoked a big

5

cigar. Then he walked across the high hill and got the best job he ever had in his life—work on the railroad section. He held this job for 23 years. Walked 5 miles to and from his work. His highest wage scale while he worked was $3.06 per day. He paid for his farm by working on the section and improved his fields by working at night in the moonlight and by lantern light.

In the meantime, my grandfather Nathan Hylton came to live with us. He was past 70 and I was 14 when we built a house of logs where we lived for 29 years. Grandpa and I cut down oaks, scored them with double-bitted axes, and hewed them with broadaxes. We split rock with wedges and hewed the big stones and built the chimney.

Then I found work in Greenup, Ky., where the town was paving its streets. I got a job as water boy for 75 cents a day. Very easy work for me. Too easy. It was hard for the foreman of the paving company to get a man to pour cement into the concrete mixer. I asked for the job and got it. I was 15 then. I did as hard a work as any man, for I held the job, which more than a dozen had quit, until the streets were paved.

It was there I saw my first high school— Greenup High School, where well-dressed boys and girls walked leisurely on the streets. And I wanted to enter high school. With somewhere between 22 and 30 months of schooling at Plum Grove, I took a Common School examination on 11 subjects. Four of these subjects I had never studied. I had to make an average of 75 and not below 60 on any subject. I made an average of 78. I made 59 on Composition, but I passed into high school anyway.

High school was the greatest place in the world to me. Five miles to and from high school. And that fabulous game of football. Tackle a man so hard I'd scoot him back two or three yards. Lift him up and throw him. Shoestring tackle 'im and watch him fall and hold to his legs so he couldn't rise again with the ball.

At first I was afraid of this school. But after I got inside and experienced the sympathetic feelings of pupils and teachers, I thought Greenup High School was the most wonderful place on earth. My English teacher would even let me read from 6 to 12 themes in her class at a time. She even said one theme, "Nest Egg," was funny, and laughed until she had to wipe tears from her eyes. "Nest Egg," with only 6 words changed, was published 23 years later in *The Atlantic Monthly*. Also it was reprinted in Watt-Cargill's *College Reader* and is read by many college students today.

Mrs. R. E. Hatton, my English teacher, introduced me to Robert Burns's poetry. She gave me a book of his poems. I wore this book out as I carried it with me wherever I went. If Burns, a plowboy in Scotland, could do it, I, a plowboy in Kentucky, could do it. That's the way I looked at it. My high-school library and my textbooks introduced me to the Concord Group of American writers. I loved Whittier, worshiped Emerson. I read everything I could get hold of written by Whittier, Emerson, and Thoreau.

Read my first novel, *Silas Marner*, and

reported on it for my English class. I read Jack London's short stories and loved them. In high school I made my way by hunting at night and following a trap line to and from high school, selling animal pelts and possum carcasses to anybody who would buy. In the spring months I dug wild roots and sold them.

At the end of four wonderful years in high school, I went back to the farm. I had written more than 100 themes and 200 poems for Mrs. Hatton. And I had read many books. They had lifted me. I saw beyond my Greenup County hills. I wondered about the world beyond. I talked to my father about going to college, but he wouldn't listen.

One day, when he was working on the railroad sections, I drove the mule team to the barn. I went to the house and packed my clothes and themes. I told Mom I was going. I hated to hurt her. I thought she would cry. But she didn't. She laughed and said, "Go ahead. You'll be back. Chickens come home to roost."

I was off to the big, wide world of America. And I was on my own. First, I got work with a street carnival. Here I met people. But I lost this job somewhere near Cincinnati, Ohio. I gave too many free rides on the Merry Mixup. From here to Camp Knox. From Camp Knox to the steel mills, where I spent almost a year and learned to be a blacksmith.

And it was in the steel mills that I became acquainted with modern American writers: Robert Frost, Edgar Lee Masters, John Gould

Fletcher, Carl Sandburg, Edna Millay, Malcolm Cowley, Sterling North, Sara Teasdale, all the then-known modern American poets. When September came again and the leaves colored I had my debts paid, a few dollars ahead, and I left the steel mills. The year was 1926. I was on my way to find a college.

Hitchhiking on the highway I passed Morehead State College. The place looked too big. At the second college, Kentucky Wesleyan, in Winchester, I stopped and asked a student who was mowing grass on the lawn, how much it would cost me to go to school there for one year. "Three hundred dollars," he told me. That was too much for me. At Berea College I stopped, and the dean asked me a few questions. Then he said, "We have a waiting list. Come back next year." I told him I was going to college.

It was he who suggested Lincoln Memorial University, at Harrogate, Tennessee. I hitchhiked there. Fell in line the day students were registering. They accepted me. I didn't have a transcript of my credits and I had only $29.30. Tell me, where on earth but America can one find an opportunity like this?

When in college I received $2 from my home. My people couldn't send me anything. Not with the sister and brother next to me now in high school. My mother had to help them all she could. I stayed at Lincoln Memorial three years and two summers, worked half a day, went to college half a day, graduated with a B average. I did all kinds of work at Lincoln Memorial University—farm work, sewer lines, water lines, carpenter work, crushed limestone for the roads, dining-room work. I found this play-work after the kind of work I'd been used to doing before I entered college.

Little did I know on the day I graduated from Lincoln Memorial University that 21 years later I, the author of 13 books, approximately 1500 published poems, approximately 300 short stories, would stand on the same platform and receive an honorary degree of Doctor of Humane Letters. This was something I accepted with gratitude, yet with the deepest humility, since a number of men, about my age, rose in the audience and cheered. They were my classmates and I wasn't sure just who should receive honorary degrees.

They had come to Lincoln Memorial when I did, and at that time they didn't have money or a decent suit of clothes. Today two are vice-presidents of insurance companies. Among them are doctors who have built their own hospitals in remote regions of Kentucky and Tennessee where there were no hospitals. Many are educators. This happened in America. It made me realize, if I ever realized any fact on earth, that America was a poor boy's country. That he could rise to unlimited heights if he were willing to work, if he had reasonable intelligence and good character.

When I returned to my home county from Lincoln Memorial University, the first college graduate in my family, my mother and father were proud of me. So were my brothers and sisters. I had paved the way. Two of my brothers died, leaving one brother and three sisters.

Later my father's dream came true. He had four teachers from his five living children, three of whom were college graduates. The fourth had a year of college. All were high-school graduates. We are just one among thousands of American families where this has happened. We didn't let the chances come to us. We didn't wait for them. We went out and found them. They are in America for all who are willing to look.

I was a teacher in a one-room rural school, a high-school teacher, high-school principal, and later Superintendent of Greenup County Schools. When I was elected Superintendent of Greenup County Schools my father rejoiced. To him this was the greatest honor any of his children ever received. When my first book, *Man With a Bull-Tongue Plow*, a collection of 703 poems, was published, my father couldn't understand. He didn't nor does he today understand books. To him books are secondhand life. And when people spoke to him about this book and others that followed, he'd turn the subject to my farming or my teaching. He couldn't read my books and he wouldn't sit still long enough to have one read to him. Maybe he was a little embarrassed. In his day and time, he didn't have the chance to go to school. His rural school was 8 miles away and he was a weakly child.

Then another thing happened to me for which I shall be eternally grateful. There was a family who came to America by the name of

Guggenheim and they made some money in America. They put this money to a good cause. They gave, and still give, more than 100 fellowships each year to students in various fields from research to creative work in the arts and sciences. I applied for a fellowship, and got it for creative writing. I didn't know the Guggenheims. Not even a descendant of the family. I didn't know a member of the board who selected me. I was given $2000 to spend abroad. I didn't have to report how I spent this money. I didn't even have to report what I had written.

After 14 months among the different nationalities of Europe, whose antecedents had made America, I returned to my America with this feeling: I never knew America until I went to Europe. The Europeans were fine and hospitable people. But their opportunities were so limited as compared to ours in America. I wondered what would happen if the young men and women in Europe had the chances America offered. I had the feeling that the majority of these young people would not have to wait for the opportunities which might never come to them, but they would be able to go out and find them.

Now, I realized America didn't owe me a cent. I owed America. I owed thanks to over 1,000,000 Americans who had bought my books. I owed thanks to book reviewers who had given me valuable criticism and praise and who had helped me to become a writer. I owed more than I could ever repay to my teachers, elementary, high-school, and college. They had lifted and inspired me to do bigger and better things. I was indebted to editors of magazines who bought and published my stories and poems.

I was indebted to the editors and publishers of my books. All of these people had contributed to make me a writer. Not that my father's work had not been honorable, but if I had been born and brought up in many countries I had seen, I would have followed the occupation of my father—while in America a man can choose his own profession.

I returned to America on the Countess Savoy. When we passed the Statue of Liberty, if my arms had been long enough to reach from my ship, I would have hugged her neck. America is the dream. America is the place. America is it.

Miss Elta Cooper and her class in the autumn of 1917. Jesse Stuart is at the extreme right of the bottom row.

THE ONE-ROOM SCHOOL WAS ACCELERATED TOO

Today, the one-room school, where one teacher taught all first eight grades, belongs to an age gone by. In portions of our state, especially in the East Kentucky mountains, we held onto the one-room school longer than other states in America, unless it was the mountain areas in West Virginia, Tennessee, Virginia, North Carolina, North Georgia, and northern Alabama. Still in the mountains of East Kentucky and West Virginia there are areas which are using the one-room schools. These schools are isolated mountain areas where modern highways have not penetrated, where youth cannot be transported by bus to consolidated schools.

Now, in Greenup County, Kentucky, our pupils have been transported by bus to consolidated schools for eight years. Many of the old one-room schools have been torn down and used for scrap lumber; a few have been converted into country churches, while others have been converted into dwellings. There used to be 82 one- and two-room schools in Greenup County and now only two of these are left. One, the Claylick School Building, which I visited as a young county school superintendent back in 1932, is still left standing because Greenbo State Park has purchased the grounds. This schoolhouse is now a show place. And, the other schoolhouse is Cane Creek School, where my

15

sister Sophia began teaching when she was eighteen and I began teaching at seventeen. Since I have told my experiences here—Lonesome Valley School in *The Thread That Runs So True,* many of the readers of the book have come to see this old school building. Other people, older ones with a nostalgic longing for the past, who have never read *The Thread That Runs So True* nor heard tell of the book or its author, drive to this school, sit in parked cars, look at it and dream! They get out of their cars and look in the windows at the pot-bellied stove which is going to rust and at a few of the old seats that are still left.

These people fondly remember the age gone by. And I remember the age gone by too, after having gone to one of these schools and obtaining in it all the elementary education I have. I remember them so well that with the permission of the Greenup County school superintendent I hauled the old seats where my pupils sat in 1923 to a building on my farm where I have them stored. On many of the seats I have found carved initials. I am glad they are on the seats now, but it wouldn't have done for me to have caught a pupil carving his initials on a seat in 1923. Initials are all that a few of these youngsters left to remember them by. In this landlocked and poor economic area, youth back in 1923 had little chance of higher education or making a mark in life. They had such small chance of improving themselves. Today, they have equal chances with youth over most of this country.

Now with highways penetrating approximately 90 per cent of what used to be inaccessible mountain areas, school busses can haul pupils to large consolidated schools. This new consolidated school, with better educated and more sophisticated teachers, better health practices, and more recreational opportunities is quite a contrast to the old one-room school. One teacher can teach his or her special grade without other pupils listening in. Often one grade is divided and subdivided and there are several teachers. And there is a principal, an assistant principal, and a second assistant principal, not one of whom teaches a class; there is a guidance counselor who doesn't teach but who steers pupils in the right direction according to the results of his testing. We used to talk about Big Business! Now we can talk about Big Labor and Big Schools. Business, labor, and schools are Big! They are going to get bigger, no matter what we say.

No wonder people, after a few short years in our county and other counties in Kentucky and other states, are taking their children to see what a one-room school looks like. If you ever visit one of these schools with your younger generation, who just simply can't understand how school was conducted by one teacher in such inadequate little dilapidated buildings, you will never hear a pupil say he would like to attend school in such a building as his parents attended. And the youth must wonder why parents are so sentimental over these little schools, still holding a few relics for today's youth to witness the age gone by. Although in our county we have the old Claylick

School in Greenbo State Park, a move is on by the Kentucky Historical Society to move the Cane Creek School to this park too. The older people, parents and grandparents, remember with nostalgia their school days where so many of them obtained all the education they ever had. Today the parents who attended the one-room schools have their children transported to the consolidated elementary schools where there is no expense except for lunch. And if the pupils say they can't buy lunch then lunch is furnished free to them! After an elementary education in consolidated schools, they are transported to large and growing high schools. If they can't buy lunches then they are furnished free! After secondary school education many get help if they want to go on to college.

I have traveled in 54 world countries, and I have never seen such educational opportunities in any country on the part of the earth where I have visited, (and this includes every country in Europe) as America offers her youth. And, yet, with all the free opportunities offered them, in my state, Kentucky, we have 56 per cent dropouts between the first and twelfth grades while the national average is approximately 44 per cent. In Japan the national dropouts between the first and tenth grades is three-tenths of one per cent.

Maybe there is another reason why people today in our area and others have a nostalgic feeling for the one-room school which has disappeared into that by-gone area of American life, like the ox cart, sled, horse and saddle, horse and buggy, the rubber-tired fringed surrey, the jolt wagon, express wagon, the hug-me-tight, the bull-tongue, cutter, bottom, and hillside turning plows. Even the passenger trains are going and we are taking to wings and to the fleet-wheeled auto over our broad intercoms that thread this nation. Everything has changed in restless America, a restless race, which is the only country in the world that is self-sustaining. But there is another trait in the American, a very valiant trait, which certainly belonged to Americans of past generations which is and has been the secret weapon in building our country to what it is today. **AMERICANS LIKED TO WORK FOR SOMETHING.** No matter what is said to the contrary, they still like to do it. Americans like a challenge more than any people I've known on the face of the earth.

Today, in this country, youth gets up in the morning and rides to school by bus. His books are furnished; a free lunch is furnished for the asking. Now the contrast in their going to school in today's modern elementary, junior high, and senior high consolidated schools and our going to the one-room school is that we had just the absolutely necessary things given us; we had to work for what we got. And working for an education was something most of us enjoyed, for we realized something we would work for had value. Then, there were some other features the one-room school had which the consolidated elementary school cannot give its pupils.

One of the fine features was walking to and from school. Then, the roads were not crowded with automobiles. We walked over hills and up and down valleys where there were only footpaths. And in July when our country school began, we walked barefooted along the dusty footpaths. We got caught in summer rainstorms. Often we got soaked. We waded streams barefooted. We got to know the names of wild flowers, shrubs, different species of trees. We had books in school (very few) but there was another kind of book all of us read, Earth's Book, which was filled with many pages and many delightful paragraphs.

Autumn along these paths was more interesting. The acorns dropped like big brown heavy raindrops from the oaks; the chestnuts dropped to the leafy ground from their satiny burrs that pricked our bare feet. The pawpaws ripened after the first frost. And the trees were loaded with persimmons which we tried to get before the possums got them. Then, there were hickory nut trees everywhere. Mornings we left home very early to try to beat other pupils who traveled the same path to the chestnut trees, pawpaw groves, and to the hickory nut trees. We didn't race for the persimmon trees for there was always an abundance of this ripened fruit on the ground. We couldn't finish all that fell from the trees. And we couldn't carry, although some of us tried, persimmons in our pockets like we carried chestnuts and hickory nuts. We also gathered white and black walnuts and cracked them between rocks under the trees.

I remember animal and bird tracks in the

snow. Winter was a great time too. I couldn't keep from tracking a rabbit, fox, possum, mink, or weasel. And I learned how hard it was for animal and bird to live in winter on the scanty food left for them, most of which was covered with snow. Many times I tracked a rabbit to a shock of corn on a hillslope which I shook with my hand to watch the rabbit run out. Many times I found a covey of quail hiding under falling grass where they could gather a few weed seeds to eat. I learned a little about rain and snow storms that I couldn't have learned on a school bus. But the pupils today who ride school busses are not to blame. This has happened in our changing world. We were the more fortunate because we could walk to and from school. We had two sets of books, those we used in the schoolroom and Nature's where we read the landscapes spring, summer, autumn, and winter. Each season we had to change Nature's books. We didn't go to school in the springtime but we were out working on small hill farms and there we knew the springtime too.

Anybody who ever attended a one-room country school walked on footlogs over the streams and waded the streams barefooted. He walked the paths up and down hills, around ridges, and up and down valleys. Today he will tell you of his experiences of getting to and from school before he will tell you about his experiences in the schoolroom. These are dear experiences that will never come again to them nor to their descendants who live in a world that has had a change. Youth who visit the few old school relics, bird and bat filled belfries where there used to be a school bell, who now sit and sigh at these educational items of the past, do not know what they have missed in our changing patterns of American education. I know that I saw so many things which I stored into my storehouse of knowledge that today I can still write stories from these experiences. I never want these experiences to die. But they will die unless we who have had these experiences write about them now.

No one fought harder than I did to see our one-room schools go in Kentucky and consolidated come. Mine is a written record in *The Thread That Runs So True,* also in numerous articles I wrote and speeches I gave. A country must progress and must move from the past into a modern world; our schools had to move in this direction. But this does not keep us from reminiscing over what has been with nostalgic feelings of the past when we made all we could of what we had. That was a day and time too when education was considered a priceless gift. And what is wrong with such an idea today? Such an idea in a youth or a community, a state or a nation cannot be outdated. The love and joy of learning is as dateless as Time for us mortals, no matter where we are and the country in which we live. And back in our little one-room schools, when and where we sought knowledge, was the same situation that I have seen in other parts of the world where I found youth who had fewer educational opportunities than we have in America and yet education for the youth was held as a sacred trust and was on the rise.

The rural school I attended was approximately three miles one way from where we lived in W-Hollow, but going up and over a big hill it was less than two miles. Today this little school, Plum Grove, is no more. It was consolidated into the Argillite Elementary School and today school buses transport youth from the Plum Grove hills to Argillite. I do not envy these youth who ride a school bus; who have a certain seat where they must sit and ride to and from school. They cannot run for the pawpaw patches, the persimmon and hickory nut groves, and for the giant chestnut trees where the ripe chestnuts dripped down like chocolate drops to the leaf-carpeted ground from their satiny burrs. No more chestnut trees for they, too, due to a blight, have gone into our past American heritage like the horse, buggy, wagon, farm plows, and the one-room schools. Gathering chestnuts along a school path is a memory now. This is life that will never return.

And the teacher who taught all the grades from one to eight in six hours is a memory too. When I make a speech and tell the young today about this, many of them laugh. I know what they are thinking. But they do not know what I am thinking and I do not tell them. How many of them could go to a blackboard before the school group and the neighbors who gathered in to watch the contests which we held every Friday afternoon? How many of them could work in an arithmetic match in any form—multiplication and division of common and decimal fractions— and in diagraming sentences, and in spelling. It always comes to my mind—I would like to see some of our Plum Grove youth diagram sentences with you, spell, or work arithmetic against you in a contest. In our short months of schooling we gave our best. Learning was wonderful. We had but few detractions—no radio, no TV, and not a sports event to attend every night or thrice per week. We got fun out of learning. We enjoyed it. And yet one teacher taught us all. If we got an inspirational teacher in one of these rural schools we did things since one teacher taught all.

Once after my book *The Thread That Runs So True* was published, I was asked a question that made me think. It was this: Why did so many youth from one-room schools amount to so much in life? And I couldn't deny this. It was true. And I've pondered over it since. Of course, we had our dropouts then as we have them now. We had those who didn't like school. But the great majority did like school. And, since pondering over the situation, because at one time Greenup High School, which was an independent city school, had one-fourth of its pupils from Plum Grove, we led the classes. We made the football team. We beat Greenup High School in baseball while we were grade pupils in Plum Grove. We had a tied ball game and it went sixteen innings, and Aaron Howard, our pitcher, went all the way. We beat them 7 to 6. We played baseball not softball. We had a teacher, Everett Hilton, who taught us and coached us. For 32 years now he has served in Kentucky's State Department of Education.

What I believe we had then in the one-room school was what is called today "The Accelerated School Program." If one was already alert and eager to learn, there was no problem. If one were not alert and eager, to sit in this schoolroom and hear others recite in classes ahead of him and behind him alerted him. He had to learn to study when there were others reciting or he had to study at home. I remember when I went from one grade to another in my scanty time of schooling at Plum Grove, I almost could have skipped the grade ahead of me. I had already listened to others ahead of me in their recitations and discussions. My brother, James, who attended the Plum Grove School, went in a grade and finished it. When Plum Grove ended in January, he walked over the hill to Greenup Elementary and enrolled in the grade to which he had been promoted. He finished another year in Greenup with excellent marks. Then, he returned to Plum Grove after his promotion in Greenup to another grade. When he was ten years old he entered Greenup High School and finished when he was fourteen. In his last year at Greenup High School he made all A's and read all the books in the Greenup High School library, including the encyclopedias. He got his early training in the accelerated one-room school of Plum Grove.

The youth of today who attend departmentalized consolidated elementary schools should never sigh when they look on one of the relic one-room schools now on exhibit in state parks. They ought to be informed on what transpired between pupils and teachers in these one-room schools. They should know of the many prominent Americans of the past and in high places in America today who came from them. They served a day and time in America and they served it well. And many who finished these one-room schools would have gone on to high school in their day and time had there been high schools. Many did go to academies, such as the Berea Academy, and worked their way there. From the few city independent high schools and the college-supported academies they went on to college without scholarships where they worked their way. Today, these people who worked for an education hold the highest positions in America. And they came originally from that little one-room school where one teacher taught all eight grades. Education to them and for them was idealistic and the greatest thing they could procure in life! They were willing to work for it since it was regarded as something of permanent value and the highest attainment in life.

THE PROFESSOR WHO DIDN'T LIKE ME

I knew my professor at Peabody College didn't like me. I was quite sure this was a fact. He was about six feet tall, slender and always a well-groomed man. He didn't speak with precision, but he did speak with caution. I suppose we were opposites. I couldn't figure him out. He figured me very easily—a semi-raw youth, energetic, blustery, over-talkative—full of notions and dreams—a 225 pounder, who never grew physically or mentally tired and never had enough money to buy himself enough to eat. My clothes were never as neat as the professor's.

But this professor took a strange interest in me before I ever had a class under him. He called me into his office once during my first summer at Peabody College and asked me a number of questions. These were historical questions. One of the questions was what I thought about Andrew Jackson. I told him Andrew Jackson was great because he acted first and discussed it afterwards. I told him I liked Andrew Jackson because he was a fighter and a doer, and he fought only when he thought he had to fight. And that he was one American President who didn't mind a fight he believed was right and just, before he was President and after he became President.

This professor may not remember asking me this question. But he has a retentive memory, a good mind, a durable mind—and I believe he still remembers. Time now is slipping up on him as it has slipped up on me. Only I don't believe Time has grayed his hair as much as mine. And he is old enough to be my father.

Now, in a couple of weeks after the professor I was so sure disliked me asked me the historical questions and a few others, he invited me into his office again and asked me the same questions.

"You asked me these questions before," I said. "But I don't mind answering them again." And I did. I wondered why he was trying to probe me. He may not remember this today. But I believe he does. He's not the type to forget—even to forget as long as he lives.

My second summer at Peabody I took Philosophy of Education under this same professor. I dreaded this course under him. I knew we wouldn't agree on anything. I knew he'd be probing me. He had a keen eye that looked at one with intent, full of meaning. But I wanted this course to improve my teaching. I was a teacher who loved teaching and this was why I was spending my summers at Peabody College—a school I regarded great for teachers and teaching. This was why I'd gone there last summer. I even contemplated a master's degree in education, which I never got. I never had time to write a thesis. I was too busy with creative efforts.

But from my earliest days—so far back I could hardly remember—from the time I learned to read and write—I had a hobby of trying to write poems and put stories on paper. I wrote hundreds of poems and numerous stories. Now my poems and stories were beginning to be accepted in America's best magazines.

My professor who didn't like me was being accepted in magazines also. He called me into his office to show me he'd been published in *Harper's*. "A good magazine," I thought. "He must have something on the ball."

But in his Philosophy of Education class, he asked us to write a paper on our philosophy of education.

"I'm too young to have a philosophy of education," I told him after class. "I don't have one yet. But I hope to get one after more years of teaching. Would you mind if I wrote the philosophy of my uncle who had an eighth grade education, who read *Rise And Fall Of The Roman Empire* while the weeds took his corn. He sat in the shade and read."

"Wonderful," he said. "Go ahead and write it. Sounds great!"

I wrote my paper in a single evening and part of the night. And when our professor selected one paper to read in class out of a class of eighteen, he selected my paper. He read it. There were varied reactions. Living on scanty rations at Peabody College, I decided to send this controversial paper my professor liked to a nationally known magazine, one that is still being published, to test it. I never had a quicker acceptance. And it was a good check for that day and time, one that relieved the financial pressure on me at Peabody College for that memorable summer.

This professor was the only teacher I ever

had at three institutions of higher learning to recognize a prose piece of mine, a short story if you please, as worthy of publication. And he wasn't an English teacher. English teachers I had never did suggest publication—but many stories I wrote for them—approximately forty-three—maybe a higher number—nearer fifty—were published after I left these institutions. Why was his judgment so acute?

But to sell my term paper for a good fee—which meant three meals per day and good food—I thought it called for a celebration. The men in my family had always celebrated with a good cigar. This was a good ten-inch cigar. I purchased one, lit it up and took off in full stride to tell my teacher. I didn't know he was such anti-tobacconist. He chased me from his office with a book. I'm sure he would have struck me if I hadn't got out of his way. I ran like a turkey. I wouldn't have fought my professor for anything. He was about the size of my father. I could never imagine ever striking my father. But, tobacco in my home was never an issue. My father often smoked cigars. And my mother smoked all her life. I saw nothing wrong with smoking a good cigar—especially after I'd sold a Peabody class paper to a nationally known magazine.

Now, here is the strange thing. He arranged for me to meet the most talented young musician on the Peabody campus. She was a concert pianist, I believe. There was nothing wrong in his getting us together—except that it didn't work. It didn't work for her and it didn't work for me. She was as lovely a young woman as I'd ever met. He surely selected a fine young woman for me. We laughed and talked—had a nice date and talked mostly about our professor. She respected him. So did I. But, I couldn't figure him out.

But being born in the high Kentucky hills where our music was folk music, "old time music," my taste was different. I didn't know why. I'd never cared for "popular music" too much—and I never went overboard for "folk music" or "old time music." I liked semi-classical and classical music—and every recording I ever purchased was one of these.

But I couldn't imagine myself married to or even dating a concert pianist. And I'm sure with the respect I had for this young lady and the respect she had for me—for we were miles apart—she felt the same way toward me. We were two individuals—two worlds—and worlds apart, but with admiration and respect for each other's dreams. Maybe my professor won't remember this, but I think he does.

My *Man With A Bull-Tongue Plow*, 703 sonnets, was published before I terminated my education at Peabody College. This was followed by other books after I no longer went to Peabody College. Then my professor began to review my books for the two big Nashville newspapers. I couldn't believe it! He gave me excellent and discerning reviews!

Since, I have never departed from the city of Nashville and its two large institutions of higher learning, Peabody College and Vanderbilt Uni-

31

versity, both of which I attended with a moderate degree of success (I never knew my grades at Peabody College for they were not made public) but I often return to Nashville, for a visit to both college and university. I was born among the hills—and the closest town, 1,200 people was five miles away—I used to say if I had a "home town" as so many people boasted, it was Nashville, Tennessee—450 miles from my home. I used to know every street in Nashville. So, I have made from one to two trips to Nashville for years.

Now my professor was publishing books and I was publishing books. He was writing historical books—one, *Home To The Hermitage*, which was about Andrew Jackson. And I could understand why he asked me those questions about Andrew Jackson years ago. Only my professor was reviewing my books and I wasn't reviewing his books.

When I returned to Nashville many times I was his guest. In his home no one was permitted to smoke. I could understand now why he chased me from his office when I walked in celebrating my sale of the term paper I'd written for him by smoking a cigar.

On one of my visits to Nashville when I was his guest, he said to me: "What do you know about the Guggenheim Fellowship?"

"Not anything," I replied.

"I think if you applied for it you might get it," he said. "You've written two fine books, *Man With A Bull-Tongue Plow* and *Head O' W-Hollow*."

I took his advice—applied for a Guggenheim Fellowship and got it.

Here was a professor of education—not English—who had advised. I'd had professors of English, but not one had advised me to apply for a Guggenheim Fellowship. And on this Guggenheim Fellowship I returned to the land of my father's people—Scotland—where I lived fourteen months—a land from which I went over Europe and visited twenty-eight countries on two thousand dollars. You had better believe I was frugal. While in Scotland I prepared a book for publication—which was my third book and published before I returned to America. My Guggenheim Fellowship and European travel were more than a college education.

Now I began to see the professor at Peabody College, who I was sure wasn't really warm to me, in a different light. He'd not been the close man, the extremely friendly and the glad handshaker. But he was a positive man and a doer. He did not wear his heart on his sleeve. He was a different type of man.

My books followed in succession and I taught school, was principal of a city and county school system—and superintendent of a county and city school system. And this Peabody professor reviewed my books. After my marriage, my wife, Naomi and I visited him and his wife in Nashville, although I couldn't smoke my pipe or a cigar in his home. And there were moments then when I wanted to smoke.

World War II came and I was in it and my books continued to flow and my Peabody professor reviewed my books. His books flowed too—I only purchased but never reviewed. And the years following the war now number twenty-six. And last year he reviewed a book of mine. I don't know how many of his students' books he has reviewed.

I do know my Peabody professor, Dr. Alfred Leland Crabb, is still going strong—I do not profess to know his age—but I'm sixty-four and he's old enough to be my father. But I do know of his influence on my life and I call him great. Last year when I spoke briefly in Nashville he was there.

Dr. Crabb loved Andrew Jackson. I think if Andrew Jackson had known Dr. Crabb he would have loved this amazing man—a man who wears well with all ages—from the young to the old—and he is a man who would have worn well in any age. I am happy to be one of his students and to learn finally what a friend to me he has been. What other teacher I have had or known has done more?

THE LITTLE PENCIL REMINDER ON MY DESK

On my desk is a little pencil that will not write. Still I gave it space on my piled-up desk. Occasionally, I pick it up just to read a name and date and two words of this great man's philosophy. I should respect this great man whose philosophy is said to be that of our Western World.

In his native land and favorite city, where I have visited often since 1938, I walk where he once walked, worked, talked and lectured. I have laid my hand on many ancient stones and I have wondered if the ancient tools used by his hands once chiseled them—for he was a stonecutter. He did this to make a living. He didn't get paid for being one of the greatest philosophers, leaders of men in thought and action the world has ever known.

On my little pencil, about four inches in length which is half white and half red, are three small words of Socrates, 470-399 B.C., "Know Thy Self."

What nice, thoughtful words, ever to put on a pencil. I had put a few words up in my office when I was a high school principal. I had these words:

"Know Thy Self"
"Control Thy Self"

by Socrates.

35

And I added:
> "Be Thy Self"
> "Improve Thy Self"

and

Thus, Socrates was always a part of my high school and my home. His birth 2438 years ago and his death 2367 years ago, go back into the dawn of distant time, a time mostly forgotten except by those who were great thinkers, creaters and artists, who gave us heritage that has come down to us. To think Socrates' name is on a little pencil (it is on several books among the ten thousand in my library) on my crowded desk. It is where I can see it often to remind me of a friend. One whose philosophy neither I, nor any other person, has been able to achieve. "Know Thy Self" and "Control Thy Self." I knew if and when my high school students let these words soak in and tried this they would never be problem students in high school—but they would be enlightened and progressive. They would be leaders, inspired by the words of a philosopher stonecutter who lived over two thousand years ago and never knew what his influence on a future world would be. These words could be so great for all the citizens in our America in 1969. How different our country would be if these words were known and attempts were made by each individual to let them enter.

IF I WERE SEVENTEEN AGAIN

If I were seventeen again, I would want to live on a hill farm. I would want to grow up where there are trees, meadows, and streams. If I couldn't live on a large farm, a few acres would do. But I would want space to hunt over, with a stream or lake nearby where I could fish.

I would want to mow the meadows with a span of horses or mules and haul the hay to the barn on a hay wagon. I believe that the boy or girl who hasn't ridden on a hay wagon has missed something in his youth. If he hasn't smelled new-mown clover, he has missed the finest wind a youth ever breathed.

In the spring of the year, if I were seventeen again, I'd want to take long walks in the woods. I'd want to get acquainted with all kinds of birds, how they build their nests and the kind of materials they use, what color and size eggs they lay, from the hoot owl to the chicken hawk and the sparrow, and how they feed their young.

I'd want to know all about the animals—foxes, possums, coons, rabbits, skunks, mink, groundhogs and all the others. I would want to know what they ate, where they lived, what animals were friendly to each other and which were enemies. This is a world every teen-age boy should know. And I would protect each non-destructive animal, each non-destructive bird. I would want to know the hunting laws, abide by them, and help restock and protect the game so it would be here for the next seventeen-year-old when he came along.

I would also learn the names of every kind of wild flower and plant that grows in the woods. This is a big undertaking! Few know more than a third of them. I would also want to learn the kinds of trees, so that when I touched the bark on the darkest nights I could identify the tree.

I'd want to fox-hunt on April nights when the trees were leafing and to hear a pack of hounds running the fox. I would want to own at least one hound dog and have him in the chase. A boy seventeen who has not stood on a high hilltop under the stars or a bright moon and listened to the music of barking hounds has missed a really great experience.

In summer, if I were seventeen again, I wouldn't want to miss working on a farm. I wouldn't miss plowing and harrowing land, planting seeds in the ground, hoeing vegetables, and plowing the young green corn. I would want to work shirtless, and whenever possible, bare-foot. The feel of loose warm dirt to one's feet, and their not being imprisoned in shoe leather, are good things in one's growth.

I would, if I were back at seventeen, learn all I could about caring for and building up the land. Beyond having a general knowledge of how to grow everything on the farm, I would want to specialize in growing one particular thing. I'd also specialize in raising a certain breed of cattle or a particular kind of hogs, rabbits or chickens.

And I'd want pets, too—a coon, groundhog,

or squirrel. Or I would want a pet hawk like one I once had that flew to the places where I fished and sat in a tree above me until I flipped a minnow from the stream. These are things which, after one leaves seventeen, he never forgets.

I would try to build my body strong. I wouldn't drink anything intoxicating. I wouldn't smoke until I got my growth. While I was seventeen I would want to build my body strong enough to accept the wear and tear of the years ahead.

I'd want to build my body so strong that if I were ever *forced* to use my fists they would have the power of a kicking mule. I'd want to have the strength to lift the end of a small saw log or to carry a green crosstie or the hind carriage of a joltwagon. A young man rejoices in strength, and he can build strength by proper work and recreational exercises.

And here is something I definitely would do. I'd go to high school. The boy or girl who hasn't finished high school has missed a great deal. It doesn't matter whether a person leads his class or not, whether he's the best athlete, or the most popular pupil. I never had these honors, and I failed three subjects during those years because I entered high school unprepared. But going to different classes, studying different subjects under different teachers, and getting to know the boys and girls in the school—these are things I am glad I didn't miss. I wish I could live over those four years again.

I'd try out for all kinds of athletics until I

found the one game where I could play best, if I were seventeen again. But I wouldn't miss athletics. This kind of experience builds men physically and teaches them sportsmanship and to give and take. Athletic games should teach them not to be overconfident in victory and how to accept defeat graciously.

I wouldn't want to ride to school in a bus or car, either, unless I lived too many miles away. I would want to walk to school because it would build the muscles in my legs, because I could breathe fresher air and my brain would be more alert for my studies. I could also meet people on my way, and see trees, flowers, birds, and animals, and all of these help in one's education.

This was one way I used to get my themes. I'd sit down on my way to school and write a theme after I'd seen something that gave me an idea. There is a whole world of subjects for themes that one can get just walking to and from school.

If I were seventeen and had not already done so, I would identify myself with the church of my choice and I would be there at least once each week. I once received a shocking report when I was pleading before a circuit judge for four of my schoolboys who had knowingly disobeyed laws. Said the judge: "Ninety-six per cent of the young men who come before me do not attend any church." I learned that of the four boys with me, all from good families, not one was going to any kind of religious services. These boys had missed something important.

I would be honest to the penny. Why build

strong bodies at seventeen, and stunt the great growth of character? If I were to choose between a strong body and a strong, honest character, I'd certainly take the latter. I'd want to have a reputation for honesty. I'd want to be able to go to my home-town bank and borrow, if need be, without anyone else's signature besides my own on the note. When a seventeen-year-old can do this, he has character. And if he has character, he will pay that note if it takes his hide.

If I were seventeen again, I would earn my own money, or most of it. I would take days of work for other people. And when I accepted a job from the other fellow, I would do it well—so well that he would want me to work for him again, and others who had seen my work would want me to work for them. I would do the work so that I would rejoice at the finished product and could sleep contentedly at night. We build character through work that we do with our hands. Do work well at seventeen and you'll be doing it well from then on.

If I were seventeen again, I would stand up for my convictions. Instead of being a follower of something I didn't believe and knew was wrong, no matter how popular that thing might be, I would hold out. I would be myself. I would be guided by what I thought was right. Popularity fades as often as the wind changes, but character never fades.

Seventeen may be the shortest year in your life. It was for me. It was a wonderful year in my life, a year for physical and mental growth, a year of beauty and spirit. All years are great years in which to be alive. But really, not too much happened before you were seventeen, if you will remember. You'll never again feel so much as if you could turn the earth over to see what is under it! Most of us would trade fame, fortune, and achievements for what you now have. So hold seventeen and live seventeen while you can. It will never come again.

THE IMPORTANCE OF READING IN THE LIFE OF MAN

From his earliest beginning, man whoever he was and in whatever part of the world he was at that time, learned the art of communication with signs, signals and vague forms of symbols. In tropical and semi-tropical countries, I can imagine our human species without clothes, going into jungles hunting fruit and berries to sustain life. I can imagine one group going, with another to follow. The first group would leave some sort of emblems scratched on the sand or in the caves to show the way they had gone. Not only in jungles did this happen. It happened in the caves on the Sahara Desert. It happened in what we know today as France by primitive man who roamed the wilderness searching for wild animals for food and their skins for clothing. It happened in what is known today as Italy, Greece, China, Mexico, Peru and on the North American Continent. We cannot go back a million years with our ancestor's communications, but we can and have gone back thousands of years by finding frescoes and written signs on dry cave walls where they have been preserved from rain, sun and the wind. We do know our ancestors communicated from the very beginning when they roamed the earth like packs of wild animals in search of food and shelter.

43

It is my belief, judging from what I have read and what I have seen with my own eyes, that sign languages which communicated to various groups of primitive people were developed simultaneously in many parts of the world. From these primitive means of communications languages finally came into being. Have a look at Oriental languages today. Each word is a symbol. There are many Chinese dialects. Mandarin Chinese was and is spoken in Continental China, while in Taiwan, Taiwanese, an almost entirely different language, is spoken. In each of the provinces of Continental China, dialects are so different, it is hard for the people to understand each other. Japan, an Island Empire, where words are also symbols, has an entirely different language. And the most difficult language of all, the Korean Language, which also has its dialects, almost parallels the languages of two Indian tribes on the North American continent. In all of these languages words are symbols.

Moving westward from the Far East, we go through many different language changes. India has her hundreds of languages and dialects, where various primitive people sprang up and used sign, symbols and almost undecipherable letters, that improved into communicable languages as centuries and millenniums passed. One of these languages is Bengali now used in East Pakistan, once a part of India; another prominent one is Urdu used as the major language in West Pakistan.

Still moving westward, we arrive in the

countries of the Near East. Here symbols change again. The Arabic script, which I believe originally was begun by making marks on desert sands in or near the mouth of caves where the wind would not blow them away, were the signals left for travelers who followed. Traveling on the Sahara desert sand was most difficult until the invention of the airplane to fly people over these vast wastes. Still, Arabic, that most difficult of languages, exists, a language in a constant flux of change, and no wonder for it has to change. My Arabic students speak a different language today and they cannot read nor understand what is known as Classical Arabic. Spoken in Iran today, old Persia of yesterday, is Farsi, an easy language to learn, a language with strange letter symbols that make a word, and words make sentences and sentences make paragraphs like we have in our own English language of today. Farsi may have been the more immediate language of our early ancestors, the Indo-Europeans and Aryans, who marched westward to settle what is known as Europe from whence so many of our ancestors have come to this North American continent.

Our ancestors came to the North American continent bringing with them many languages but greater numbers came bringing the English language, which was developed from many languages on an island country approximately as large as Pennsylvania and Kentucky combined, with the upper portion of the island country where Gallic was and is still spoken and the western portion where Welsh was and is spoken today.

Here I have deviated from my story on the reading communications and its importance in the life of man. Let us go back to that energetic race of world traders and doers, the Phonecians, who occupied all of what we call Lebanon today. They were what we term a Semitic Race. We often refer to the Jewish people as being Semitics. They are not alone. There are Moslem and Christian Semitics, too. I know, having lived and worked among them. The Phonecians moved up from the Persian Gulf area, where heat was intense, to the cooler and more beautiful area along the east coast of the Mediterranean Sea. No one knows except by excavations today how far the Phonecian Empire extended. But the people themselves were great sailors and their ships plied the known and unknown seas of their day and time. They had to communicate with many people and they made great strides in communications. They saw the need for an alphabet from which they created an easier and more stable means of communication.

While I am not an authority on languages and early communications, I do know the movement was always from the East toward the West. From Greece, a most intellectual country, civilization rose to a height. No other country in the world equaled Ancient Greece then and few if any have reached their civilization since. The Greeks borrowed much from their eastern neighbors, the Phonecians, and from their southern neighbors, the Egyptians. They returned all they borrowed with compound interest in thought and learning in practically all the arts known today. The Greeks reached the stars in creativity. Athens became the eye of Greece ... but let us say Greece had many eyes ... and Athens was the larger and more illuminating one. From 'The Rock', which is the Parthenon and Acropolis, came the highest thinking to help civilize a world. Our own democracy began with Socrates, Plato, Aristotle, Pericles and others at 'The Rock'. It spread to the western world. A little later, Greece's neighbor on their west, the Roman Empire, subdued little Greece. The Greeks taught their conquerors but never took away their strong language, with its highly developed alphabet, grammar and sentence structure. This Latin language influenced all European and Western languages. We call languages which are derivities of Latin our romance languages. Teutonic is the mother of our own English language. From Latin comes French, Italian, and Spanish.

Books from the Greek and Latin languages have been handed down to us, in which may be found what are regarded to be the greatest communications of man's thoughts and beauty, enough to show us who live in what we call a civilized world today (and this I doubt very much) the great power of communication in the written word. How wonderful it is that we can translate the past communications into our own words and that we can read and understand them.

How unfortunate it is for us that less than ten per cent of the Greek's great culture has come down to us; the remaining ninety per cent was destroyed in useless wars of Greeks fighting Greeks and by Greece's neighbors warring on the Greeks. How unfortunate it is that Roman soldiers put the torch to the great library of Alexandria, Egypt which was established by Alexander the Great to rival Athens, the cultural center of light in a darkened world. How unfortunate it is that not all the poems of Latin and Greek poets have not come down to us. How unfortunate it is that those early communications from Europe back eastward in all those many and varied countries, different races, different national cities, have not come down to us. But how could those very early primitive sign and symbol languages ever get down through the centuries and millenniums to us? We of today would like to read these and communicate with our distant ancestors. Can you imagine what their thoughts were? What did they eat? Surely they developed signs and symbols regarding food. What did they think of the elements, places of abode, death and the afterlife?

We can only make conjectures about and dream of what has been lost and which we can estimate conservatively to be approximately ninety-eight per cent of all past creativity. Our ancestors have been on the face of our earth millions of years, so our anthropologists estimate. Recorded civilization, of a most highly civilized people, the Egyptians, goes back about fourteen thousand years. Egyptians did not impart all their ancient wisdom to us. Much of this died with the Egyptians, due to useless wars and invasions, similar to those which destroyed Greek culture and the highest civilization known to man. But we must be thankful for that less than ten per cent, luckily to have survived and passed down to us so that we can communicate with Pericles, who loved his Athens, and Socrates, the greatest man who ever walked on earth and a stone-cutter by trade. I always like to know what great thinkers and artists do on the side to make a living. Our country today pays them and my guess is these who are paid, become fat, rich and lazy and do not produce art. I am not the first to say this. William Shakespeare said this in so many words and many implications, centuries before I have said it here.

Then, there lived the great Aristotle, Plato, Demosthenes, Euripides, Aristophanes, Aeschylus, Sophocles, Pythagoras and Xenophon. I mention Xenophon, because of his great book, *Anabasis*. He wrote many books but this one, I believe, is his greatest. He merely kept a diary, and due to his Athenian training as a student and scholar, and not as a soldier, he wrote this book, one of the world's greatest books. He went to Persia as a mercenary soldier along with 14,000 Greeks to help Cyrus dethrone his brother, Artaxerxes, King of Persia. Cyrus was killed, and through an act of treachery, all Greek generals who accompanied the tough Spartan army to Persia were killed. The approximately 300,000 Persian troops, who were to fight beside the 14,000 Greeks for Cyrus against Artaxerxes' army of approximately a million and three-hundred-thousand, closed ranks against the Greeks. Here is a writer's communication to show the reasoning of one man, Xenophon, and how he led a rebellious Spartan army of 14,000 through a hostile land, up through Persia to the Black Sea, across the Bosporus Straits and on to Thrace. He was two years on the road and arrived with approximately six of his fourteen thousand men who had fought all the way. What a communication in the written word this is! Had there been recording and pictures then, could these have come down to us? No wonder people in America today say something is true and know that it is because they read it on the printed page of a newspaper, a magazine or a book.

Two years ago, we saw *Trojan Women*, written 415 B.C. and first played in Athens 413 B.C. at the Epidarus Theatre. This is 1968 A.D. It is a great play and was superbly acted by an all-Greek cast and in their native language. We saw another play, *The Frogs*, written by Aristophanes in 405 B.C., in Athens at the Herod Atticus Theatre which is on the very spot of the Dionysus Theatre, on the side of 'The Rock', below the Parthenon and Acropolis. *The Frogs* had been performed here on this very spot for the first time in 405 B.C. I mention these two plays that are among many of the great communications that have come down to us; however, not one-half of the plays of the world's greatest dramatists have come down to us. We are happy that these have, thanks to the printed word which is the greatest communication between all world countries that has ever existed.

Then we ask, why should people read? We ask why our youth should develop the reading habit? What can educate a young person more than the habit of good reading in a world of books? And why do Americans seek the sordid and be absorbed by sex, when sex has always been with us? What is new about it? Why seek the sordid when the great books are too many for one reader to read in his lifetime? In great books there is some sordid sex, too, which is recorded by implication. Why are our minds twisted thus, I was asked in Korea, regarding sex in the American novel. Either sex or murder or a combination makes the best seller lists and seems to be preferred above all others by American readers.

The Korean intellectual cultural groups could not understand our taste and asked me, a representative of the U.S. State Department and sent in dual professions of speaking and writing, to explain American tastes. I had often wondered about this, too. It was something I could not explain very well, our taste in culture which we had sent around the world—a taste I doubt will live as long with civilized man as the taste of the ancient Greeks. The thought came quickly, sex is and has been with people of the world as long as there has been man. It had to be or we could not have populated the earth. America is a new country and too many of our people are just discovering there is such a thing as sex. This certainly brought the laughs from a mixed audience and the Koreans felt satisfied with my reply to the question that had stumped them as well as many Americans.

In my home I do not walk among my old friends on the shelves and read of American murder and sex unless they are incidental. I cannot sit for murder each evening on my TV. Such may be cultural exponents from my country but not for me. I walk among my ancient Greek and Roman friends. They are on my shelves. They speak to me. Among my Roman friends, to mention a few, are Juvenal and good old Virgil; good old Horace, Terence, Dante, Plutarch, Martia. My regret is that I waited too long to walk among so many great Greek and Roman friends. Of course, Dante and Virgil had spoken faintly to me in my youth. Homer, Socrates, Plato were merely names of great men who had whispered.

Why had I waited until I was fifty to know more of these men and to become acquainted with their contemporaries, predecessors and successors? Sometimes the child is father of the man. Our daughter, because of a Greek teacher in whose class she sat, heard him get so excited until he raised a sweat. She, too, rose up in excitement with this teacher in a class she could not take, for she had finished only two years of high school. This happened at the University of Nevada where I was teaching in 1958. Our daughter decided to know more about the Greeks and Latins, and decided then to major in the classics. And she did major in the classics with excellent grades in top universities. She sent me her books after she read them. I then realized what I had missed. Ancient voices spoke by word of communication and opened up a new world to me.

My daughter, at the old age of nineteen, suggested to me that since her father had missed these great writers—these wonderful communications from worlds that have been but still live through portions of the printed word handed down—that I, her father, who was one of four editors of a high school Literature and Life textbook, should read these classics and include a section in this book entitled, Classical Heritage, so that the youth of today attending high school would at least be introduced to this fabulous world. Today you will find this section in one of the finest textbooks ever compiled for youth; and, incidentally, that section, Classical Heritage, is one of the most read and loved by high school students, according to teachers, of any division in the book. This is how reading communications spread . . . even from parent to child and child to parent. At the age of twenty-four our daughter, who is teaching part-time at the University of Indiana in the Classics Department, has gone a step further by sending me her translations of Horace, Virgil, Archilouchus and Anacrean, which are good enough to have been accepted in the best literary magazines.

Now, who are the men and women who have long gone to their rewards but who walked with me and opened a new and an exciting world when I entered that great institution, little Greenup High School, with about 125 pupils, and yet where Latin and French made up a part of our curriculum? It was not the real ancients who spoke to me there. They merely whispered in a low voice. But Robert Burns, a plowboy from Scotland, had reader appeal for me in his beautiful down-to-earth lyrics that sang a beautiful music to the ears of this Kentucky plowboy. He made me really conscious of poetry. His poetry went around the world and even today in Russia, he is considered one of the world's greatest poets. He wrote of people in his day in Scotland like we have in Kentucky. He wrote of the poor, defended the downtrodden, and laid the poetic whip to war mongers, scoundrels and society's untouchables. He appealed to me. He walked with me. He taught me a kind of culture that money spent for culture today in America cannot buy. There was my first novel to read, *Silas Marner*, whether it is great or not, I thought it was then. Mary Ann Evans' (George Eliot) book was great for me. After Silas Marner came novels and poetry by Scott, then novels by the greatest of novelists, Charles Dickens and Thomas Hardy. English poets and novelists opened a world to me. These English authors became my friends. Today they are in our household and on our book shelves.

In Greenup High School I found a collection of de Maupassant's short stories. De Maupassant spoke a better language to me than Edgar Allen Poe, who was a favorite in our high school and with my English teacher. Reading de Maupassant's stories, without the suspense and artificial plots, stirred me deeply. Because of this one book, I wrote better themes in high school and later in college, which in later years turned out to be forty-one publications in American literary magazines, all written in high school, a college and two universities when I was a student.

So, why do we encourage our pupils to read books? Why does the hungry, searching student find his own books? He finds them because somehow, by the influence of a teacher or teachers or on his own initiative he has developed a good reading habit. When he develops a habit of reading which is a good one, an educational habit, he might even become an educated man. By his reading the printed pages of great books, he garners the best thought from the great minds of man. To garner this thought, to live, feel and to create by teaching and writing, he, too, can soar from the earth to the stars.

In Greenup High School, Ralph Waldo Emerson, a profound thinker and man, spoke to me. He seemed to say in all his essays which I read over and over: I have found a way in life. Follow me. And I followed Emerson. He said so many things that I wanted to hear. And I believed him. Today, Emerson has a place on my desk. He sits there in the covers of his Collected Works. Then there is Henry David Thoreau. He and I got real chummy in Greenup High School. What he did on so little money, living alone in a cabin by Walden Pond, prompted me to build a cabin out of crude poles, take my books there and read by lantern light.

Since another friend, Nathaniel Hawthorne, had himself a wooden platform built among the pines and a ladder going up to it, a place where he could look over his beloved New England countryside, I did the next best thing by going to a pine grove on my father's fifty-acre farm and hung my lantern upon a pinebough where I wrote my themes for my Greenup High School English teacher. Youth are great imitators. To read great books by great men is a profound guideline for imitation. Here I heard the wind on many a lonely night sough through the pinebough needles, speaking to me in a strange and beautiful language.

Then, my dear friend, Mark Twain, gave me the books I loved. I made myself a log raft and paddled it down the Little Sandy River. I did not have too many American friends, but Jack London was one of these few. I had my world of communications through the printed pages. I had another world. It was a great world that inspired me to leave my hills for more learning and more books.

Do youth receive communications today from American and other writers of the world? Certainly they do. I have proof of this as one individual and one writer. I get letters from all over America. Not a postman's day passes that I do not get them. I get letters from the Near, Middle and Far East. I get letters from Europe, Canada, every state in the United States, from South America, Phillipines, Australia and New Zealand. I get a few letters from island groups. I get them from countries all over Africa. Many of these have said: "As your Robert Burns and Emerson were to you, so are you to me". It is the finest feeling in the world to receive such letters.

They make up for all the letters which have damned me, mostly from the ignoramuses who have never read my books because they are non-readers, yet who gather from word of mouth and implication that I am ruining my state and my part of the world. Names I have been called and heard about by such people, who have not read my communications of my native land to the world and would have extended my ire, had I heard them, to an explosion from a non-violent man. These men have never walked with Robert Burns, Emerson, Henry David Thoreau, Nathaniel Hawthorne, nor Mark Twain in their youth. They have never communicated through the reading habit with the great Greeks, Romans and with great names from all over Europe and the British Isles. These are among the few. But still we have them in a land where there exists the greatest opportunities to rise to the stars.

Why does American youth not read? I might ask why American adults do not read. Why do American teachers fail to read? If you doubt me, go into the homes of teachers and check their personal libraries! See who their friends are upon the book shelves. See how many friends they have! What I have found amazes me! Yet so many teachers complain of their students not reading. If they would only read themselves and tell their pupils about the books they read. To have students read, they must have teachers who will read. Teachers should not read a book to a high school English class, but they should let students do their own reading. High School students are no longer sucklings on the educational bottle, prepared with primary ingredients. Some English teachers actually read for them. I once had a coach in McKell High School, Ben Webb, who taught history, who developed the finest group of readers among his husky athletes of any teacher I have ever known. How did he do it? He was so excited and full of the book he had just read, history or historical novel, that his students got excited too. Incidentally, he had the third largest personal library in our county, some five or six thousand volumes. Mine is approximately ten thousand, while a student Coach Webb and I taught, Lee Pennington, has surpassed us with approximately fourteen thousand volumes. He is a teacher in a state university who has no trouble getting his students to read.

There are other ways of getting students to read. Make large lists of selected books, wherein they can pursue and discover, and offer them extra bonus grades for reading and reporting on books. Why not? Why not help them with extra bonus grades, instead of cash from the government to buy culture! Help them to become avid readers of good books where they will find the responsibilities of dreams and more dreams to give them Pegasus wings to let them soar to heights they have never known before. I never taught many high school youth who haven't read *Green Mansions, Son of The Middle Border* and *Giants In The Earth*. When I spoke to teachers in well-known city school systems in the not-too-distant past, I spoke of these books. English teachers, not young ones, mind you, did not seem to know about them. Only one teacher in the group had read one of these books, *Green Mansions*. And I said: "I certainly did not teach you. You would have known about them."

Reading is the greatest communication from world citizens to world citizens of every hue, color, religious and political faiths! It is not merely ignored by today's youth. It is as rejected by our teachers and our adults as by our youth. Many of these teachers call themselves English teachers. They are paid as thus. How can they be when they communicate by ear and eye to windflashes on the screen which is with them for seconds and then, like Robert Burns said of snow flakes on the river, in a moment melt and are gone forever? Reading communications hold, they excite the mind, they tear at the heart.

I am sixty-one. I read *Black Beauty* when I was six or seven. I recall how *Black Beauty* spoke to me then. I will never forget it. The book is read still by our primary and elementary youth. I dare say they will not forget it either. Books I have read, books I have recommended and taught youth in high school and college, have become a part of me. They will go with my mind, my flesh and body someday to a Plum Grove grave. But the dream will escape. It will be there for others to see, to read, to dream and feel on the printed page as I have walked and dreamed, laughed, wept and pondered my great friends upon my shelves, in every room in my home, so I will be close to them because I love them and whatever I am, they have helped to shape and make me as they have helped to make and shape others through the centuries and millenniums.

Jesse Stuart at a teachers meeting at McKell High School.

STABILIZING A GENERATION

Try this test if you live in the country or if you live in the village, town or city. I have often challenged my high school students to do this.

Walk out alone some early Spring morning when the weather is comfortable and the streams are running full of fresh spring water. Sit on a stone, stump or log and listen to this singing water. Test yourself to see if you hear lyrics, symphonies? Test yourself for enjoyment! See if you can sit quietly for an hour!

Try on this morning walking alone under a grove of hard wood trees, soft wood poplars, beeches and ashes and listen to the slow moving winds among the tender green spring leaves! Test yourself to learn if you hear music here—if you see beauty—if you can content yourself to be alone. Above all, test yourself to know if you have time to think.

Of course there will be spring flowers in any area where you are in spring—you may or may not want to look at these. I have always sought groves of percoon on such early morning walks. I can sit for an hour looking at these flowers that grow in fertile cones—around old rotted logs and stumps.

Also on such a morning walk you will be bound to see birds, perhaps ground squirrels, woodchucks and rabbits. Where you walk beside the stream and under the trees, listening to water and wind is there natural habitat. They make

61

their homes here. You will see birds flying over with something in their bills to feed their young. Only one will be fed at the time by a parent bird—while all the other young in the nest will be crying for food.

You may even see an owl sitting half asleep upon the branch of a tree. Or you may even see a battle in the air of crows chasing a chicken hawk who has come close trying to steal a young crow from their nest for his breakfast! You will see them hit him time and again in flight—and the feathers fly while he makes his way, dodging from tree to tree to a part of the forest that is his homeland. There will be many things and places for you to see.

Make your test to be all day if you can be alone with yourself—out where no human voice is spoken—out where you hear only natural sounds and wildlife voices. I have suggested to my high school pupils they take this test, then write a theme about it—telling me what they did. What they observed and how they felt during these hours. Many of them took the test over and over again, without writing about it for they enjoyed getting away into a world not made by man—but a world man, little by little, inch by inch, either deliberately or unconsciously was out to destroy.

When you take this test in this area, if you are lucky, you might see a flying squirrel going to his home from tree to tree on his strange wings. His home is usually in a hollow sourwood or beech—and you might discover a family of the large brown woodmice that have the prettiest brown eyes I have ever seen in an animal's head—and, this will be exceptional, but you might come upon a woodrat's home—never destroy one of these, for the woodrat will never be a pest—will never be domesticated. He builds a nest on top of the ground of sticks and grass higher than your knees.

When you take this test contrast all of this with the man-made, so-much-of-the-same, over-and-over again, here today and gone tomorrow televised programs, brought into your homes to steal more of your time than you ever give to books. Contrast what you see out where you can see and listen—out where you are alone and have time to think, with how much of this you will remember and how much of the TV programs you remember.

Also make a contrast of your observations of the animals and birds you see and compare the real likenesses of them as compared to the caricature illustrations found in papers, books— where artists exaggerate to draw your attention! Why do they do it? Natural drawings will attract your attention and you won't have blurred images of these you will have to correct in your minds eye when you observe the true likenesses of these wild creatures.

If enough of you young people will take this test in the new generation of tomorrow you may help correct the incorrect teachings, exaggerations, sensationalisms that expand and expand in America—each trying to outdo the other! Even correctness now would really be radicalism. You might be going to nature and getting a true picture, stabilize the generation of youth who follow you. From a stabilized generation America can have more power and creativity than from an unstable exaggerated generation!

Then, there is this wonderful test of self—more important than any lesson in any textbook I have ever taught! It will be left to you—and perhaps you will be a dull perceptionist if you cannot take this test—if you go out, say you don't see or heed anything—that you were so bored you couldn't stand or understand all you had seen and heard—and that you will return home to enjoy your favorite programs—that you are willing to accept, love to accept, feel them refreshing and satisfying, canned artificial programs, so-much-of-the-same, over-and-over again, exaggerated, many akin to nothing you have ever seen before on earth that man has created for you to steal your time and give you exactly nothing in return.

By having such problems with my students, wasting time on such programs—our communications in America are the greatest time thief ever created by man—caused me to suggest a test that I have taken over and over again since high school days to the present.

This is a good test for you in high school! It is a good test for parents—for individuals, for everyone. Unfortunately, many of you are not close to a natural background to take this test. But you do have fast cars and good roads in America and you can easily get to this background. For heaven's sakes you go alone and don't have a supervisor! Don't have anyone to speak to you. If you do, you'll destroy the test. Do this yourself. Learn to think and be yourself. Shed off the artificiality and the exaggeration so commonplace in your great country as a duck or goose sheds water from its well-feathered body. In your growing up—and after you have grown up—you must have time to think and time to observe. You certainly can't get it from time-stealing communications brought into your home you sit and watch by the hour which you will have forgotten three days later! If all continue this, what kind of generation will we produce for tomorrow?

McKell High School

MY SEVEN SEVEN
YEAR PLANS

From the time I was fourteen, I have been fascinated with certain figures—and one of these is figure seven. The sound of speaking seven is musical to me. The shape of the figure is nice. It has angles like boughs on trees. I see more sevens among winter's leafless foliage than any other figures.

The letter has more value to me than its musical sound and its shape. Since I was fourteen I have used seven year periods in which to build my life. I was doing this before I ever heard of the Ten Year Periods in Totalitarian Countries. I heard of these later in my life while I was trying to fulfill my own seven year plans.

I didn't select ten year periods for these were too long. Ten years, too, in a man's life is too much age, I reasoned. Five years gave too little time. I had to find a figure between five and ten— and since I like the figure seven, I chose this one.

From fourteen to twenty-one my plan was to finish high school and write a book. I fulfilled these two ambitions under great difficulties. I did more than fulfill these objectives. While I grew from boyhood fourteen to manhood twenty-one, I had learned a trade, being a blacksmith. I had military training and I had taught school. The book I had finished was a collection of poems which I called *Harvest Of Youth*. I had finished three-fourths of my college work to earn a degree.

In the second seven years I planned to finish college and get my first book published. Anything else I might do beyond these objectives I considered bonuses. At twenty-two I had my degree. At twenty-three my *Harvest Of Youth* was privately published. I had many bonuses in this productive second seven years plan. I did four summers of graduate work at Peabody College. I did a year of graduate work at Vanderbilt University. I had written, but didn't know it, enough material for a collection of stories, *Head O' W-Hollow,* at Lincoln Memorial University before I graduated there. I had written a term paper at Vanderbilt University, *Beyond Dark Hills.* Later it was published as my third book, not counting *Harvest Of Youth,* because it had been privately published. I also became the youngest county school superintendent in the Commonwealth of Kentucky, which was a nice bonus. My first big book, *Man With A Bull-Tongue Plow,* was published in this period, the second seven year period which was a great bonus. My first big short story was accepted and published by a story magazine. An added extra bonus was winning the Jeanette Sewal Poetry Prize.

At twenty-eight when I entered the third seven year plan, I had planned to buy as much W-Hollow land, land my parents had once rented and farmed, as I could. I was certain to have two more books published, *Head O' W-Hollow,* stories and *Beyond Dark Hills,* autobiography. I planned to continue as principal of McKell High School. I also planned to make America's "Big Four" magazines,

Scribner's, American Mercury, Atlantic Monthly and Harper's with short stories or with poems or with both. This was before Esquire magazine was born.

This seven years plan turned out to be more exciting than the last seven years plan. Instead of having two books, *Head O' W-Hollow* and *Beyond Dark Hills* published, I had four books published— *Men Of The Mountains,* my second collection of stories and I wrote my first novel, *Trees Of Heaven,* which was accepted and published. But the great surprises that happened in this period were the extra bonuses!

How great was life! How great it was at this time in America to live life fully—I was recipient of a Guggenheim Fellowship—I sailed for Scotland. During fourteen months in Europe, I visited twenty-eight European countries. I came home and married Naomi Deane Norris, a classmate in Greenup High School. I received a $500 award for *Men Of The Mountains* from the American Institute of Arts and Letters. I bought approximately one-third of the land I now have in W-Hollow. And just as this third seven year plan ended, a real nice bonus came to Naomi Deane and to me: our daughter Jessica Jane, our only child, was born.

At the beginning of the fourth seven years plan, we were engaged in a shooting war with Germany, Italy and Japan. Naomi's back had been broken in a car wreck in Mexico while she was pregnant. Now, she was still wearing a brace. I remained out of the war awhile and could have stayed out indefinitely—but I couldn't do this. I had written books, one a novel, *Taps For Private Tussie*, which won the Thomas Jefferson Memorial Prize of $2,500—and it was selected by Book-of-the-Month as a single selection and sold over a million copies. I made the "Big Five" magazines, Harper's, American Mercury, Atlantic Monthly, Scribner's and Esquire with stories and poems. My bonus magazine was the Yale Review. I took "boot training" in the U.S. Naval Reserve at Great Lakes. I was trying to make Seaman First Class when I was commissioned Lieutenant (Junior Grade). My bonuses of extra published books in this fourth seven year plan were: *Album of Destiny*, a big book of poems; *Mongrel Mettle*, a satirical commentory on our times, only I used dogs instead of people; *Foretaste of Glory*, a novel; *Tales from the Plum Grove Hills;* and *The Thread That Runs So True*, a book on teaching. This was a rich and rewarding fourth seven years plan. I had done more due to my being in service than I had planned to do.

In my fifth seven years plan, I had dreams of maturing and excellence. *The Thread That Runs So True* was voted by the National Education Association as the "most important book of 1949." Then following this publication came a planned book, *Hie To The Hunters*, a novel, and *Clearing In The Sky*, stories. Also published during these seven years were *Kentucky Is My Land*, poems; *The Good Spirit Of Laurel Ridge*, a novel; and *The Year Of My Rebirth*. It was in this fifth seven years plan that I knew frustrations. I lost my mother and three years later I lost my father. I came down

70

with a near fatal heart attack—was most of one year in bed and most of a second year convalescing. My thoughts were during this period: Try to get my health back again. I was two years building strength. Then I returned as principal of McKell High School—a step backward which I have cause for regrets. The school had fallen apart. There were problems and frustrations in this fifth seven year plan.

My sixth seven year plan began with the planned publication *Plowshare in Heaven,* a collection of stories. Then, I was asked to go to American University in Cairo, Egypt, to teach. I was to teach in AUC, Naomi in The American School in Maadi, a suburb of Cairo, and Jane was to enter her freshman year in American University in Cairo. While I was teaching there *God's Oddling,* the biography of my father, was published. A great extra bonus came to me. I was awarded the $5,000 Fellowship of the Academy of American Poets.

The first bibliography on my work, by Dr. Hensley Woodbridge, was published. Two more books were published, *Hold April,* poems, and *A Jesse Stuart Reader.* And in 1962 I started on an around the-world tour for the United States Information Service (U.S.I.S.), "the right arm" of the United States State Department. Naomi went with me as far as East Pakistan; when her parents were killed in a car wreck she returned home and I went on around the world—my greatest single achievement—lecturing extensively on Dual Professions, Creative Writing, and Teaching in

Egypt, Greece, Lebanon, Iran, West Pakistan, East Pakistan, the Philippines, Formosa (Republic of Free China) and Korea. Ending this sixth seven year period my 300th short story was published in Free Press, Manila, Philippines. I regarded this, having my 300th short story published (all stories had been published in quality magazines) as three milestones (one for each one hundred stories). This achievement was an extra bonus—one I had worked for. I regarded this one as an excellent bonus—one I had never planned to do.

In my last seven years, my seventh seven year plan, I made big plans in advance. In these years from 1963–1970, I finished buying all the land I wanted to own in W-Hollow—all my parents had ever rented, plus a few other acres—which totaled approximately 1000 acres. I had added these acres to the one acre I traded possum hides for when I was fifteen.

I decided to do more travelling. Naomi and I travelled back over Europe. Again we travelled in Northern Africa and Europe and around the continent of Africa—which made Naomi's having travelled in forty-seven countries and I in seventy-five countries. Travel to us is recreation-education.

During these seven years, I have been associated with Eastern Kentucky University. I go, lecture and teach, part-time when I'm called on.

Books published in these seven years were *Save Every Lamb, Daughter of the Legend, My Land Has A Voice, Mr. Gallion's School, Come Gentle Spring*—and another book due this autumn, *To Teach, To Love.*

Our biggest bonus of this period was our first grandchild, Conrad Stuart Juergensmeyer. Then a living monument, the Jesse Stuart High School, Calley Station, a suburb of Louisville, Kentucky, was named for me. When it is eventually completed there will be 3200 students and it will cost over six-million dollars. This really pleased me as a top bonus.

Extra bonuses during the seventh year plan, something I never dreamed or knew would happen, were four books written about me and published—Dr. Everetta Love Blair's *Jesse Stuart: His Life and Works;* Lee Pennington's *The Dark Hills of Jesse Stuart;* Mary Washington Clarke's *Jesse Stuart's Kentucky,* all published in 1968. Ruel Foster's *Jesse Stuart* was published in 1969. And Dr. Hensley Woodbridge's *Jesse and Jane Stuart; A Bibliography* was published July 1969—and what a bonus to have daughter, Jessica Jane, capable of doing Greek, Latin and Medieval Italian translations and having them accepted and published in quality American magazines—also having her own short stories and poems accepted in high-level magazines, to the extent, now only twenty-six, of having her included with me in this Bibliography. What father wouldn't be proud of such a daughter?

On the reverse side of this late part of my seventh seven years plan, I have had a light heart attack, with which I was hospitalized in Intensive Care and from which I am home convalescing. I have also had a "left bundle branch block."

Now, I am making plans for books in my eighth seven years plan. I am writing a book. I have plans for three others, perhaps four, already written to be published. I have ideas for four I plan to write, I plan to continue with being on Eastern Kentucky University's faculty, and plan to lecture less over the country. We have plans for more world travel.

Not considering my six junior books already published and the seventh to be published in the Spring of 1970, I hope to have from one to two new adult books published each year—one by each of two major publishing houses. My aim now is to push my poems beyond the 2000 publication mark and my published stories to The Fourth Milestone (400 mark, from which I am not far away now). There is much to do and so little time left. Life is a race and I have been a runner through each of my seven year plans.

Life has been exciting from the one-room miner's shack where I was born near the entrance of a coal mine to the home where we live now, a mile away in W-Hollow—a home listed by Kentucky's Heritage Commission.

Naomi and I never plan to stop growing, working and living as long as we can. I have high hopes, especially in publications for my eighth seven years plan. I hope there will be a ninth seven years plan. And there could and might be this plan. It will take this time and more to do what I would like to in my living on this earth. I want to leave something of value for others. Even the little ground squirrel buries an acorn and it sprouts, grows and becomes a giant oak with its top against the sky. Man should be as ambitious as a ground squirrel.

CHARACTER AND THE
AMERICAN YOUTH

Character and the American youth is a subject dearest my heart after my many years in the schoolroom, teaching hundreds of youths in secondary schools and after speaking to approximately 40,000 university students and members of teaching groups in America.

We have, since the beginning of history, had citizens who were demoralizers and debasers of youth and character. Why did God speak to Moses on Mount Sinai and give him The Commandments to deliver to His people? These Commandments have changed the course of history in morals and character. They are a moral and spiritual code for us to live by.

If all the people in America lived by the Ten Commandments, I wouldn't be here speaking to you on Character and the American Youth. We would have the most powerful nation this world has ever known. Because good morals, character and integrity are decendents of these commandments.

There are two forces in this world. There is the force of good and the force of evil. We belong to one or the other. There isn't any neutral side. These two worlds grow and spread and combat each other. They have done so down through time.

So many people make the mistake of trying to get somewhere too fast. There're no shortcuts to morals, character, integrity and hard work. When I went into the Navy in World War II, I tried to enlist as an officer. My father said, "Jesse, you're starting at the top and you're liable to go down." I failed a physical, the first and only one in my life, and went into boot training and fought to be a seaman 1st class.

After I had visited 29 foreign countries, I'd like to add that any youth, willing to work and sweat, can be honest in America, make a living and accumulate. You will never know your America until you have visited foreign lands where there are limited opportunities.

Here is one of the greatest mistakes parents make today. I mean parents who have had to struggle. They don't mean to hurt their children. They think they are helping them. They never want them to work as hard as they've had to work. They want life to be easier for them.

Children should know that the good things in life come hard. It's a sin to raise a child up and not let him learn how to do work with his hands. Let him earn money and guide him to spend it wisely.

The American, and this is another story, is the greatest worker I've seen in any of the world where I've been. Then, why shouldn't our youth work? We say they're lazy. I don't say it. I know better. Before World War II, only 300,000 high school youths had jobs on the side. Today 1,500,000 have jobs and attend school. Throw American youth a challenge and they love it.

We in America haven't everything over the

Europeans. Try to find a pile of tin cans on a street in the towns of Denmark, Finland, Norway and Sweden. Look over Germany. You find clean cities. We need to clean our cities and build parks. There's work to be done in America. We are not the cleanest people in the world. We should take time from bragging, to clean America up.

Graduates, you will soon be leaving Baylor University. Each of you must travel to your destiny. You are the finished products of your homes, your elementary and secondary schools, your churches, and Baylor University. The Kingdom of God is within each of you. You can only travel on one of two roads. One leads to neutrality of living and to nothingness. The other leads to certain destiny of fulfillment. This means you combat evil forces, that you strive to build a better country for your children to grow up in.

TIME AND A PLACE FOR GROWING UP

There is nothing more needed today among our youth of secondary school age than time to think. Instead of giving them this we have been putting more and more pressure on them, giving more quality to, and expanding, their curriculum. I know this is an American trait in business, in about everything we do—even now in education. We have a tendency by our fresh virility and exuberance to overdo, once we get started, in anything we undertake. Now in education we show tendencies to over-educate those who are young, who need a few lazy years while they grow in body and mind.

In my last year as McKell High School principal, I ran into this. First, there was rivalry, as there is and will always be, anywhere, anyplace, anytime among high school students. This rivalry is not always caused by students trying to get scholarships but it is something innate in young Americans. They work to surpass one another. Each wants on top of his or her class. If one can't get top honor, then second place is second choice and third place is third choice. If he or she can't be first, second or third, then it is the "upper three or five or even ten per cent" of his or her class. Ambitious students work and work for this.

A greater problem at McKell High School was among parents who pushed their children beyond the breaking point to do something the parents had never done, were not too concerned about doing and couldn't have done when they were high school students. I was in a good position to observe and measure results, for in McKell High School I had been teacher and principal before and had formerly taught approximately eighty per cent of the parents. Even the parents came to me saying their children's grades were not as high as they should be because so-and-so's son or daughter had made higher. They pushed their youth almost to the breaking point. We did have a small percentage to go beyond that point. We had a few "disturbed youth" as a result of rivalry and mostly because of their parents pushing for them. It was like parents rooting for our school's football team on which their sons played.

Here an idea occurred to me. I think it is a good, safe idea, one that could never hurt, but could only help. If we had had the space, I would have tried out this idea.

The idea was not new with me. I came upon it in Taxili, which is east of Rawalpuidi, West Pakistan, where I observed a university that had flourished in about 200 A.D. Archaeologists had uncovered this university upon a slope overlooking the broad valley that different civilizations had occupied for short and long periods in history—each civilization had held it for a time, had been defeated by clashing armies, had lost, had been pushed out and replaced by another. Today archaeologists find this one of the most fertile sites of an ancient civilization. Second to the National Museum in Egypt, here was the most interesting museum I had ever seen. Here were relics of high civilizations of millenniums past, toys our youth could use today, jewelry the beauty of which our women in America had never seen, and the weight of which our women anywhere in the world would not want to carry. The proper jewel regalia for the well-dressed woman went up to forty-two pounds. All of this high civilization—with the ruins of a university in its midst.

No one lived here now. The winds swept over the broad valley where most ruins were still underground. The ruins of one city had been uncovered, and while observing the ruins of this old university, I heard a piper higher on the slope above me playing a flute for the goat herd he was guarding.

Now, of the education that had come from here, not anything could be seen in the museum. I would have liked to have seen their books. I would have liked to have seen their school library, their furniture. I would have liked to have sat down with them, nearly two thousand years ago in their dining room, which had been excavated here, and I would have liked to have eaten a meal with them. Almost two centuries would have been a broad credibility gap between an ancient civilization when might made right, and our present civilization when we are flying on metal wings over the earth and sending missiles into space. (In retrospect, we know we have not, in our present day, advanced beyond "might makes right." We have its presence everywhere in our world today.)

But what interested me here was something I observed that would help our youth in Kentucky—youth who have been pushed to the brink of exhaustion with school studies and extra activities until they have no time of their own. They have not had the time to grow up. Now the peoples who had once lived in this ancient city were closely akin to the oriental civilizations from antiquity to the present, which take more time to grow up and live than do western civilizations. In this university there were cells, perhaps used by the teacher who was likely a Buddhist monk. Perhaps he had a few students around him in this windowless cell. Perhaps one student occupied the cell. No one knows now. There can only be suppositions. One man's imaginative supposition about these ancient educational methods and procedures is as good as another. And ideas came quickly to me here on this fertile spot where ancient learning had once flourished and where so little information, not even the name of the college or university, had been left to posterity.

But I was positive they had left one clue that would help me today in our western world with our youth. If I could only have used it in McKell High School! I would have had rows of small rooms with ventilation but no windows, where each youth could have sat in the light by switching on a light or in darkness if desired. He or she could have taken a book or left a book.

Each would take just an hour each day all by him or herself to give some time for growing up. Call this subject GROWING UP. Make this an accredited course. If she or he would sit still, ponder and have dreams, give grades according to conduct. There should be more A's given in this course than any other. This would, I believe, out there in the unforeseeable future, have more influence on students than any course given in our high schools.

Since I didn't have the physical set-up for this in McKell High School, I did the next best thing. Many schools do this, too. Provide for students one quiet study hall per day. In this hall the student will have quietness, yet about him would be others. The student wouldn't be completely isolated. I think the student should be completely isolated for at least one hour.

In this area, in my day and time, I had the time left for me to grow up. I had so much isolation that I constantly desired company. I never grew tired of my classmates. I walked five miles to school and five miles home. Students can't do that today, not if they want to, due to dangers along our crowded highways.

And where are there places in overcrowded cities where students can go and be away from people for an hour? They live in apartments or in dwellings on lots with but a few feet to separate each home. They play on playgrounds filled with youth! They cannot walk on paths on ridges and in valleys like I did. They cannot walk alone beside the streams and rivers and hear the winds in the willow leaves, spring, summer and autumn—or hear the winter winds blow lonesome through the leafless willow wands in the winter. Youth in America miss something by not being able to take long walks alone over the countryside.

There in Taxili, as in my Kentucky, one had time to grow up, to dream and to think. Since all the high school youth in America cannot have such opportunity today, I think a substitute place should be furnished for him or her in the high school. Giving each student this new opportunity, giving him rest and relaxation, I believe will work wonders. In our surge now to overeducate, we are pushing our youth to the brink—perhaps to mental disorder or physical disaster. Let us relax for a change.

POVERTY OF THE MIND

Millions of dollars are being spent in Appalachia, my region of America, to provide food and clothing for the destitute. The poor are helped all over America—and costs run into the billions of dollars. We know about "our poor" and we should know about them. Helping the poor has been on the lips from those seeking the presidency of the United States to those running for constables. Each wants to have a part in this popular program. It has gotten publicity not just over the United States but in about all countries in the world. Our plight, especially in Appalachia, has been singled out and likened to a pumpkin's shriveling on a withered vine. Perhaps, there are some countries in Central Africa, the more backward ones, where people don't know about Appalachia's plight. But Americans have done a good publicity job of giving our poverty to the world.

In 1949, twenty years ago, my book *The Thread That Runs So True* was published. There was a paragraph in this book where I spoke of my area's being dormant while the improvements and movements in education, from first grade to university graduate levels were sweeping America. This is still true. It is true we do have poverty for want of proper food—and for the necessities of life, clothing, better housing, better everything—roads, schools, churches and public buildings. We have poverty all the way around.

And I like to include in this we have poverty of the stomach.

But the greatest poverty we have here, and in other parts of America, is the poverty of the mind. If we didn't have poverty of the mind, we wouldn't have so much poverty of the stomach. And there are those beyond Appalachia who think the only thing to do with Appalachian youth (especially the boys) is to give them vocational training and send them off to industrial plants and factories in the North. These youth, when trained in vocational education are exceptional workers. But to think of sending all is definitely wrong. Here are some of the finest minds I have ever taught. I know the people of Appalachia! I am one of them. I've taught them in high school and university and I've taught in other areas of the United States and I've done foreign teaching in the Near East. The finest minds I've ever taught have been Greeks from the Greek Islands, Greeks, Armenians from minority groups in Egypt and countries of the Near East and Moslem girls from Egypt and the near East who are now just beginning to have the opportunities to be educated. The minds of Appalachia are nearest to these. The minds of Appalachia, generally speaking, are far ahead of Appalachian hands. Their trained minds make doctors, lawyers, teachers—they are great in the arts.

What is needed, instead of always keeping Appalachian poor and the people victims of the handout checks, is to establish better schools, academic and vocational—like everybody else in

America—throughout all of Appalachia, an area which comprises one full state and portions of seven others. We need especially to establish better elementary schools to feed better high schools and then to feed better colleges and universities. It is the poverty of dormant minds, not yet awakened that is stymieing us in Appalachia.

Do you believe a college graduate in Appalachia will let his yard be in a graveyard for old wornout automobiles? Do you believe he will throw bedsprings, tin cans and garbage in the streams? Don't you believe he will have too much pride to do this? And what about high school students properly taught—do you believe the majority of them would do this? I don't. It will be that tiny minority who is slow to respond to education that will desecrate houses and landscapes. Don't you believe if a college graduate lives in a coalcamp he will paint his house? Don't you believe to eliminate poverty of the mind through education first is the answer? I know it is. It will never be the answer to end our plight by sending in outside missionaries to help direct and the feeding of the poor with Government and State subsidies.

People of Appalachia are not dumb. They are not trained in comparison with youth outside of Appalachia who have better schools and better everything. Give the youth of Appalachia now better educational opportunities to eliminate poverty of the mind. Train their minds and their hands and in a very short time Appalachia will move upwards to new heights. Citizens of Appalachia will be paying taxes into the United States Treasury instead of subtracting subsidies from it. I know of nothing more tragic than mountaineers who are untrained, who have no work, who live in Appalachia, a land so unsuited to farming, having to bow and bend for a pittance to survive on a small Government check—just enough to hold soul and body together. The people I know want something better.

A program for better schools, inspirational teachers, and courses to provide for all opportunities is the answer. This program should be now! We have waited too long. We need that school program to eliminate poverty of the mind. When a high school principal tells me only thirty per cent of his school's graduates are going to college—when he thinks this is a high percentage at this time in American progress, I know something is wrong. At least fifty per cent should go to college while the other fifty per cent should have training skills in other professions. We will have poverty of the stomach far into the future at this rate, for we are not eliminating poverty of the mind.

Our Appalachia must have a new face. We must have better housing, but the new wage earning Appalachians would be able to build new homes. In owning and living in new homes, they would clean up the face of earth around them and protect their streams to make them clean and to beautify them again. The educated who remain will create new small industries. They will do this on their own as the New Englander and the Midwesterners have done. With Appalachia being a more attractive area, with better schools, roads, better everything, and with a supply of workers trained in various skills, large industries would then want to move in. But behind all of this progress, has to be one thing—better schools, better teaching, and expanded curriculums.

Nationwide and worldwide publicity about our Appalachia would soar, paralleling a foreign mountainous country, which has done as well, if not better, living among their mountains, than their neighbors in the plains. This country is Switzerland, from which our Appalachia can also learn some valuable lessons.

In natural beauty, West Virginia, the only one state which is all Appalachia, is called "The Switzerland of America." Let this not be merely beauty in which we are comparing to Switzerland, but let it be in the training of skills, industries, cleanliness, learning and enlightenment, Switzerland is the eye of Europe in progress. Let Appalachia be the eye of progress in America. We can do it with new and better education as our foundation stones. We can build unlimited from this foundation.

MEMORY ALBUMS

I believe that a man can memorize a rosebush full of blooming roses, for here is a beautiful picture complete within itself. It is just as complete as "In Flanders Fields," by John McCrae or "I Have a Rendezvous With Death," by Alan Seeger, World War I poems I memorized in Greenup High School from 1922–1926. I have never forgotten these poems. They are written in words which I have memorized, and many other poems too; and words and lines in these poems form pictures in my mind which I could see when I recited them forty years ago or recite them today. In these poems, I see the same pictures forty years ago and today. Thus, along with words, I have memorized pictures! Isn't this true with most readers? Aren't we very much alike in so many things we do?

Now, to memorize a rosebush in full bloom is a beautiful image to store in the mind. It has never been recorded in words nor has it been painted. It is a memory piece put away—stored in the mind!

I know that I have memorized hundreds of natural objects that have never been photographed, painted, or written about in words. I cannot help doing this. I see an object which interests me. Sometimes I stand and look at it. Sometimes I don't. I just walk on. If I were a painter I would never get all the pictures I have stored in my mind painted.

I have memorized my entire valley. Anywhere I go in the world I take a picture of my

91

valley in my mind—down to the smallest details. If ever a test were given to me on how accurate I am to the details I retain in the memory of my valley, I believe I would make an exceptional score. I have memorized all of my farm. Outer edges of these thousand acres may be a little dim and vague in my memory pictures, for I have not seen these acres often enough. My valley and my farm are long picture-poems I have memorized.

Now, in regard to some of the shorter object-poems I have memorized. So many of these have been trees. Often these trees change in growth or they are twisted and disheveled by lightning and storms. To see them again plays havoc with that memory of mine that once photographed them to perfection. This is true of country footpaths. I used to walk over paths and loved them. They became pictures in my mental album of recorded photographs. Perhaps in one year or two years a path can change. And in the deep dark woods where wild animals have made a path—say they got killed by hunters and the path is no longer used—it goes back to the jungle again. A path can go back to the jungle in five years, never leaving a single trace.

I have memorized waterholes for the cattle in dry pastures. These can change in a season. But a waterhole in a dry pasture is a beautiful mental photograph, one that remains indelibly in the albums of the brain—even if the waterhole changes with the seasons.

And I have memorized buttermilk skies with intermittent bright stars peeping through or with a full moon and dim stars—and these mental photographs are on a broad canvas of sky. In such mental photographs I have almost caught the sweeping high winds that bend and sway the leafy-topped trees and sing through the needles on the tall pines.

In my English classes in high school, I used to suggest little things for my students to try for personal enjoyment. Only a few smiled at me when I mentioned they try memorizing objects and storing these mental pictures in the albums of their minds. I told them this was a good enjoyable practice that made them observe more closely. Many students are so practical. Never a time I suggested this to a class I didn't get the question: "Why do this? What is the point of doing it?"

My answer: "It is good mental training. It trains your mind in detecting and storing mental images. It gives you more incentive to search for and to appreciate the beautiful. It trains your mind. Above all you can make this an enjoyable game—one which you can do alone when you are out taking a walk. This is a game, perhaps, you can do the best when you are lonely. And when you do this, you will cease to be lonely."

"If you ever decide to be painters, you'll have more mental pictures in the albums of your minds than you'll ever get painted," I told them. "If you ever visit in foreign countries and you get homesick for scenes at home, all you'll have to do is sit down and in silence go through the many pictures you have of your homeland. If you're at home, and you want to see winter when it is summer, springtime when it is autumn, all you'll have to do is pull the pictures from your mind. You will have enjoyment with your storerooms filled with memorized mental photographs."

Many of my students have gone through the years practicing storing mental pictures as they practice memorizing poems of their choices. I told them to memorize what they wanted to remember (and gave them credit) in my English classes. Many have memory albums of choice poems today in their minds which they often turn to and recite poems just for their own pleasure.

So why wouldn't the memory album of appealing scenes, the four seasons of the year stored in mental photograph albums, be essential and most gratifying? It would have to be. If you have never tried it, try doing this sometime. You will find it is a unique pleasure and that it gives great joy.

GUIDANCE WITH A HEART

Shortly after I started teaching, I adopted a philosophy that has worked for me. Each boy and girl in my classes was my son and daughter. Although I was not married then and had no children of my own, all those I taught and all those I supervised were my children. After I became a high school principal, when one of my pupils was not getting the best from a teacher, I talked to the teacher in private. I knew each child was an individual, each had the "Kingdom of God" within him.

I believed each pupil was worth all the time I could give him. I never let a pupil down. When he was convinced of my faith in him, he had faith in me. I disciplined and encouraged by persuasion, by talk and taking long walks with the pupil. I found out about his background, about himself. Often I sat on the back steps or the front steps of his good (or poor) home and talked to his parents.

Long ago I learned that teaching and guiding young people wasn't done by one set of rules, such as one might use in a store to sell products. I learned it wasn't done by grades alone—good or poor grades are only a part. But a teacher, principal, superintendent, must look forward to preparing his students for their places in the world. I looked forward to mine, even when my high school family got up to 600.

I realized that McKell High School is small, compared to some high schools. But regardless of the size, I will always take time to counsel and direct a student when the time comes for teen-age mischief.

Let me explain what happened last year to one of my senior boys. An average student, Jim had reached that stage of adolescence where he had a few wild oats to sow. Somehow, and in some way, he got himself an old car. He no longer rode the school bus but drove his own car, bringing his two brothers and sister to high school. He burned up the highways and, so I was told, went in for drag racing on public thorough-fares.

One morning his sister came to me and said: "Mr. Stuart, Jim had an awful fight. He's not able to come to school." Upon questioning her, I found out that the fight was over the superiority of two makes of automobiles in one of the drag races. Fred, the youth with whom he had fought, had given Jim a sound beating. So I talked with Fred about what happened. Fred told me that he hit Jim so hard that he had cracked his knuckles, and he thought he could feel slivers of bone under the skin. I told him to go see a doctor while I went to find Jim and bring him back to school.

I found Jim loafing on the outskirst of the village. His eyes were almost swollen shut, his face bruised. He also appeared to be a little addled. I told him I wanted him back in school. I knew why he didn't want to return—he had lost the fight and he had pride and hated to face his classmates after the beating he had taken. He weighed 119 pounds while Fred was 60 pounds heavier. Jim, as a matter of fact, was often mistaken for an elementary pupil instead of a high school senior.

Jim returned to school because I was in constant touch with his parents. I knew how much he was studying, where he went and when he got home. When I told him this he was amazed but, nevertheless, proud that I had taken so much interest in him.

Just when I thought he was getting back on the normal track, he stalled his car one evening on a railroad crossing. Jim barely had time to escape. The car was torn to pieces. I didn't tell him I was happy that he was without a car.

Less than a week after Jim's car was demolished at the crossing, he was driving the family car to take his mother to the hospital for a checkup. He was a good driver. His father, mother, brothers, and sister were in the car when an irresponsible driver came from nowhere and hit his father's car. This collision put both his father and mother in the hospital for a week. I told Jim he had to be careful, since it looked as though Death were after him. He agreed that everything he did was bad luck. I told him that, for all the bad luck he had had, he would have a piece of good luck. He expected and believed this.

But now he wanted to leave school. He would start to school and never get there. When his sister told me he would get on the school bus and then slip out the rear door when it stopped to pick up more pupils in the village, I would get in my car and go and hunt him up and bring him back to school. I went after him so many times that he tried to dodge me. I borrowed other cars he didn't know, in order to find him.

"We have 600 in this school and you waste your time on one," said one of my teachers. "We are five teachers short, too."

I didn't answer this teacher. He had been one of my pupils. I had wasted my time on him, too. He had forced me to fight him once, and he was a rough competitor. It took force for him—and today he is a fine teacher. Why should he not remember and think what I was trying to do with Jim? Jim was different. He didn't need force to guide and help him, he needed kindness and encouragement. His teacher showed me what Jim was doing in his class. Then he showed me Jim's brother's grades. They were all A's.

"That's it," I said jubilantly. "I've got it."

I was elated. His brother, Bernard, was a year younger with superior grades and he was as popular as Jim was unpopular. Bernard surpassed Jim on intelligence and achievement tests with points to spare. Jim had never surpassed in anything, never in a test. Going on the assumption that Bernard's superiority in everything had caused Jim's fights, wrecks and his wanting to leave school, we arranged a test over things we thought Jim would know. We gave this test to the senior class so the brothers wouldn't suspect anything.

The result was that Jim soared above his brother. This did it. His personality changed. He never missed another day in school. He participated in play and started working, trying to make up what he had lost.

I believe there are as many problems of

growing up as there are pupils in a school. What will apply to one pupil will not work with another. I believe teachers and elementary and high school principals cannot take too many courses in psychology. I believe all problems, 98%, perhaps higher, can be worked out and the pupil guided in the right direction to make him a good, maybe great, citizen in our society.

If a teacher or principal works for pay only, and doesn't have love for and the interest of his pupils in his own heart, then he has chosen the wrong profession. Above all, if he doesn't understand youth he shouldn't teach.

I like to go into a classroom just to talk with pupils. I tell them they can amount to something in life. It is easier to be a somebody than a nobody. This I tell them: "Somebody in this classroom will do well—not one teacher knows or can guess the right one." I tell them that not even the pupil himself knows he will be the outstanding one in his class. This is something these pupils never forget. The one who does well in life is seldom the one suspected in the classroom.

My father used to tell me that there are more ways to choke a dog than on warm bread and butter. There are more ways than one to pull the best from a pupil. When I have pupils who make low grades and cannot help it, I say something encouraging, something to stimulate them.

What I have to say for colleges and universities who will not accept the average or a little under-average pupils is another story. They destroy confidence many teachers have built up in these pupils. Many of these students who have not made the best grades in books have added worlds of horse sense to my classes and my school. This sounds like I'm all for the average or under-average pupil. Not at all. I believe in guiding and helping all to achieve the best they can do.

When pupils have left my school, whether they are brilliant, average or below average, I want them to have an A character. I tell them so. I tell them I would rather have a pupil who is a C student but who has an A character, than to have an A student with a C character. If the C character is brilliant but cannot be trusted, then his brilliancy is not much use to himself or to his society.

REBELS WITH A CAUSE

Two thousand and thirty-two years ago, there was born in what is now Venusia, Italy, Quintus Horatius Flaccus, better known today to the world as Horace. He was the son of an Apulian tax collector, who was freed by one of the patrician Horatio families from which he took the name Horace. He was educated in Rome and later in Greece. His early poems were protest poems, cruel and heartless. Naturally these would have been for he enrolled in the Republican Army of Brutus and Cassius who were defeated by Octavius and Anthony at the Battle of Philippi in 42 B.C. when Horace was twenty-three years old. He commanded part of a legion in this battle. Now with his father dead, and he a loser, all his father's property was confiscated. But a popular poet of that time, Virgil, who believed in Horace, was able to secure financial help for him through a wealthy patron, Maecenas, and it is good that he did.

There was dissention in the Roman Empire. There was dissention among the people and their leaders. Julius Caesar, one of the greatest Roman emperors had been stabbed to death. The Roman Empire, then the dominant Republic of the known world, the wealthiest and most powerful country on earth, one no other country dared fight, was having its troubles from within. The growth of young Christianity was the basis of much of this trouble. These young Christians didn't think it was right to reduce conquered men to slavery and take their wives and daughters and put them in brothels. They were rebels with a cause.

After Augustus became emperor, there was still dissention in the land and here is where the influence of Horace was so great. For Horace, a deeply religious man, was obedient to the gods he knew. He had changed from his early protest poems, his heartless poems, to write poetry of the sturdy Roman family, the great yeomanry of the land, that sturdy citizenry that was the pillar upon which the great Roman Empire drew its strength. He wrote of those who had not gone to Rome to receive positions in the Roman government. He wrote of the countryside, of ancient gods, of the people. Go back and read translations of Horace's poetry, one of the great world poets, just to see what he wrote. Horace was offered a lucrative position by Emperor Augustus but refused the offer. He stayed with his patron and continued writing to show the Romans and the world that the strength of the Roman Empire was in the families of the land, those who tilled the soil and fed the people, those who worked at independent professions, those who served in the Roman armies under the Roman colors of that vast and powerful Republic. This great writer was a rebel with a cause and he put the right emphasis on the right things. This is one reason why he is so great in a world today, a part of which he never knew existed. His power and his steadying influence was a great help to his country and to Emperor Augustus. No wonder Emperor Augustus offered this descendant of nonfree Romans a position of power.

There is no record in his writings that I have found where Horace wrote, "You held my family in bondage and now is my time to go after you since I have become one of the greatest writers in the Roman Empire and the world." Quite the contrary, for Horace tried to save the Empire in which he was a citizen. He switched completely from a protest to stability in his creativity even in an empire where the rich had become richer, where slaves did much of the work, where people of higher brackets lived softly in wealth and licentiously in lust. In fact, he tried to save an empire. Although by doing what he did he might be considered by our present-day American terminology a conservative, he was a conservative rebel with a cause. His literary works, more alive today than they were then, will prove this point.

Little did Horace know, or perhaps even dream, that 1557 years after his birth three sailing ships would sail directly west from Spain, a part of the old Roman Empire, for three months to discover a new North American continent and there, upon that continent, would someday be another republic, with many similarities to his own Roman Republic, the United States of America.

Horace, of course, didn't even dream that the United States of America would have all religions of all its citizens living in freedom under its flag, that the religion dominant in this country would be Christianity, and that this republic got enough territory and knew when to stop without trying to annex more. He would have been proud, surely, to have known that this republic could have annexed more territory without firing a shot in conquest because other people and other races would have joined us had we let them. I believe it is true that we treated the people of our few colonial possessions better than we treated our nationals. Two of these possessions joined us as states by referendum. Another possession, we just turned loose, without giving them a referendum to see if they wanted to join us. I wish this experiment, in all fairness, had been enacted with the Philippines. I would have liked to have known what they would have done. Horace would have liked our idea of never having enslaved men from conquered countries to do our work and certainly never putting the men's wives and daughters in brothels. Here we certainly differ from the Roman Empire. Our Christians and our Jews (who had been too often enslaved themselves) would never permit this.

Today our country is at war, our third war in twenty-five years of national scale, under the auspices of fighting for the freedom of other people that would, if not for us, be suppressed. But the fact is, we are at war. Another fact is, we have dissention in our land, a kind that Horace and Emperor Augustus knew in the Roman Empire. Our dissention might even be worse in our republic, a land I love and of which I am proud

104

to be a citizen. I am proud to be a citizen because, unlike Horace, I was born a free citizen but under more destitute circumstances than he because my father, who couldn't read or write, could never have been a tax collector. Instead, he was a coal miner, a railroad section hand, and a very small farmer on eastern Kentucky's rugged slopes. All I ever asked of my country was a chance. This chance was given, although I worked for it. In my belief, our government doesn't owe us a living but we owe the government our loyalty and our tax support. I feel that we who stand for this are rebels with a cause.

True, the Roman Empire, under its laws, gave its citizens many freedoms. The Romans were great on laws. We have inherited many of our laws from them. But we have given our citizens more freedom under our laws. How the citizenry reacted under freedom, under Roman laws, was a question in the Roman Empire. That is the same trouble in our land today. Why should certain elements of our population work to change our form of government from within for forms of governments of other countries, forms of government that suppress our freedom and our minds? If we should, and God forbid, ever have one of such governments over us, these people who advocate such would be among the first to rebel against it.

I am not old fashioned in my thinking when I say this. Never accuse me of being so. For I am one of America's better traveled men. I try to stay abreast not only of my own country but also of the world, in which I've visited approximately seventy countries and in which I have worked in over nine. I never thought I'd live to see in America any person or persons, citizens of this country, who would burn an American flag in public—a flag that has been and is a symbol of our great republic, our freedoms and all that we should hold dear. I never thought I would live to see draft cards burned before television cameras in Washington, D. C., the Capitol of the United States of America.

In my last year as a principal of McKell High School, one of the senior boys came up to me and said, "You know, I want to be a rebel without a cause." For days his teachers and I had been watching the pecularities of this boy, how he had changed from his normal pursuit and was now going around twisting his body and shaking his head. He had been a good solid youth, with good grades and a fullback on our winning football team. At that time I didn't figure it out, for I had never seen the movie, "Rebel Without a Cause". Very soon we had so many boys going around, mad about nothing, trying to be James Deans, that I went to see the movie that had influenced them. The trend was mad at the world for nothing. I have seen many silly pictures but this was the superior silly. Nevertheless, it influenced youth who are great imitators in the elementary and high school years. So, who was James Dean in an unimportant little role as movie maker? Well, his movie was enough to influence youth for a time. But he forgot, in his role of make-believe, that a high-speed engine could make four wheels leave the road. So he's no longer a rebel without a cause. But the "Rebel Without a Cause" influenced more youth in my school than any rebel with a cause. You know now where I got my title for this address. While James Dean's flimsy celluloid content was on the wrong emphasis, my written work here, I believe, is on the right emphasis.

When you're on the right emphasis, as you graduates will later learn, you will not get your share of the sensational publicity. Good teachers, honest workers at trades, farmers, policemen, soldiers, men of all armed services, all people of trades and professions that form the bulwark of our population such as Horace described among the Romans, are substantial rebels with solid causes. Our ancestors who built America from a wilderness to a greater republic than Horace knew and all their descendants who are trying to preserve us, were and are the greatest rebels with the greatest cause.

Note, I did not mention in all professions our religious leaders. I have to deviate here. I must make concessions. Under the emphasis of Christianity and non-violence can we cause violence to the extent of death? Something definitely is wrong. If we are real Christians we should have brotherhood. Another note on this which disturbs me greatly is the fact that too many have discovered either God is dead or that the Divinity of Christ is a myth, thereby upsetting their beliefs and youth's beliefs into no beliefs. Among the Greeks, predating Christianity, Greek gods and, later, Roman gods were very much alive. People then, as now, had to have faith above the fallibility of man on which to pin their hope. The Greeks were so deeply religious they consulted their gods before battle.

Being Christian, God the Father and God the Son are my gods. I am of a nature like millions of other Americans—I have to believe. And, furthermore, I want to believe. It is great to have a faith above man in which to pin our hopes. I could scarcely live without this faith, and the miracles, now doubted, which it contains, one of which happened to me in Murray, Kentucky. I lived with so little chance. Remember there were quarrels among Greek gods as there were among the greeks, and even gods fought each other; they married, too, and bore offspring, but they were never doubted by the race in the Golden Age of Greece that contributed more to world civilization than any race on earth. They were a deeply religious people. The Romans, who worshipped many gods the Greeks worshipped, under different names, were perhaps less religious than the Greeks; nevertheless, they could be called a people and country loyal to their pagan gods and after the advent of Christianity, loyal to and perpetuators of the Christian faith. Some of the gods might have been doubted but they were never maligned.

Our troubles and dissentions, which are coming from within, have mostly risen like vaporous clouds in the last four years. So many of us expected them to pass like morning winds blow the clouds away. But the winds have been stagnant and more clouds, that appear to be evil and forbidding, have arisen beside them. So in the land where I was born and grew from childhood to manhood, where I have worked, played, and enjoyed life and the pursuit of happiness, I now feel I am standing where a volcano might explode. And I am so scary man. I am not given to superstitions. I think my conclusions are solidly based by comparison to other countries where I have lived and worked and still many more I have visited from one to twenty times.

In Egypt where I became a temporary citizen so I could teach at American University in Cairo, I saw my first riots. Not being accustomed to governments of the Near East and to the minds of people who lived in countries of the Near East, I naturally thought these riots were spontaneous. When I learned they were planned, incidentally, planned by the government, where people were massed, cameras set up to take pictures and send them over the world for publicity purposes, I was dumbfounded. These riots usually were against America and here I was working for Egyptians and on a small salary. One of the comments I made then, along with the few other Americans who were battling with backs to the wall over Russian influence there was, "Planned riots could never happen in America. How could they ever happen in America?" This is a statement I have had to rescind many times.

Later, in 1962 and 1963, I went around the

world working in dual professions, teaching and writing, for the USIS, called the right arm of the United States Department of State. Everywhere I worked—Egypt, Greece, Lebanon, Iran, West Pakistan, East Pakistan, the Philippines, Taiwan, and Korea—people complimented me on living in a great and steady country where there were no riots. I just returned home when they started in America on a full scale. I wondered what the people in these countries with whom I talked and worked thought of us now. Our news media and magazines played this on front pages and on magazine covers. This was sent to all parts of the world. This is what foreign magazines and papers reprint on us. On my return trips I have said "this is bad about us". And I have been told, "Well, it is true, for you have said it. We just reprint what you say about yourselves." Today, 1967, I could not go to countries where I have been and speak and work with them. They wouldn't have me. Egypt no longer creates propaganda and sends to Panama to give us trouble on the Panama Canal and to other parts of the world. We create the propaganda on ourselves and send it like we would any other commodity to any part of the world that will rejoice in having it.

At a Midwest university in America, under the auspices of Christianity, youth were trained to be missionaries of freedom and what not in southern states. When at this time in Midwest America, in teeming cities and ghettos, there were conditions that warranted all the missionaries they could train and send. And from time to

110

time there are explosions in one of these cities heard around the world. In New York City, that citadel and bastion of wealth and power, which also sent out its emissaries and apostles of freedom on how-it-should-be-done, why do they have to form citizen brigades of vigilantes to move all night and patrol streets to protect citizens? Why do they have to post policemen on the subways to protect the passengers? I went to New York City first in 1935. It was a wonderful city and one could walk about anywhere at any time and not be molested. I feel safer in large cities in the land of our enemies than I do in New York. I wasn't afraid to walk anywhere in Cairo at any time of night nor in Rome, Athens, Beirut, Istanbul, Damascus, Paris, London, Edinburgh, Copenhagen, Karachi, Lahorre, Calcutta, Manila, Rangoon, Bankok, Taipei, Tokyo, or Seoul; not nearly as afraid as I would be in New York. Even in the Capitol city of our America, Washington, D. C., in a stone's throw of our seat of government, citizens had to wear masks so as not to be identified for fear they would be killed when they testified against crime.

Now is there dissention in our native land, our vast, our powerful, our great republic? I ask you if I am lying. Did the Roman Republic, and later the Roman Empire, ever have more unrest? Could you imagine the last three writers in America to receive the Nobel Prize—Faulkner, Hemingway, and Steinbeck—writing about the virtues of the solid American home, the solid yeomanry of the American people who still till the land by mechanized methods? Do you think if they had written of these they would have had top billings and best sellers? Could and would they run against the popular grain of mass thinking to portray the have-nots and the wanting-froms and never say a kind thing for the haves who have-to-give-to. Had they done this, as Horace did, they wouldn't have gone as far as they have in their day and time. With no reference to any writer, nine-tenths of our writing is synthetic. Time will show too few writing giants among us, not equivalent to the Romans and certainly not up to the standards of the Greeks. We have too many self-appointed rebels without a cause. We have too many weak-kneed phonies who are afraid to stand up and be counted for fear of not being on the popular side.

Riots and rumors of riots among college and university students, and even high school students, are among the dark ominous clouds that have risen in the past four or more years. Of course, we've had some few since we've had a country but those were spontaneous and not planned. Riots are so common, like picketing, they have become commonplace. I can understand picketing better, for in most instances picketing is for a cause—better wages, shorter hours, more benefits, and longer and more lucrative paid vacations. I remember the rioting my wife and I saw. American Peace Corps workers stood defiantly in East Pakistan against native students rioting against the government which owned the colleges. The government asked for four years of college training, like we have in America, for their degrees instead of two years. Students had been out most of the second year, had about one year of college, yet won their plea to be college graduates. I know college and university students in America wouldn't have done this. Do you think these young people are trained as well as you in less adequate schools in one-fourth the time? No wonder they have problems. They are rebels with a cause on the wrong emphasis.

When you receive your degrees, and leave Murray State University, you will go from here in your varied fields of endeavor. You either have to be a rebel with a cause or a rebel without a cause. You must be one or the other, for there is no place between where you can straddle the fence.

Sorry we cannot offer you a country at peace. Sorry we cannot offer you a country without indebtedness. Your ancestors and mine have made minor and perhaps some major mistakes, although not intentionally, but errors of judgment as you might make in the years ahead. But you are going out into the greatest republic in the world, with its war, with its indebtedness, with its internal unrest. You're going out into a country activated on all fronts in advancement and achievement. You are going out into the most virile country I know on earth. If there is one with more virility, I haven't visited it.

Maybe you can be a rebel with the cause of helping keep this country at an even tempo. Why be a rebel without a cause when there are so many

113

good causes? And the best is never burn a flag unless you have a better one. Sit at the round table and discuss, or do in a voting machine what cannot be obtained by riots and marches. Of course, by riots and marches you'll be photographed and your pictures will be in the papers and on magazine covers quicker than if you solve problems around a round table or by votes instead of bullets. With all our country's faults, and we have them, same as individuals and other countries, you are inheriting the greatest country, and I am prejudiced, in the world. I believe Horace would have liked us above all others.

Horace is very much with us. His work lives on. He was a writing rebel with a cause and his written word was on the right emphasis. What he said and did are timeless. He died eight years before the coming of Christianity but Emperor Augustus, the great Roman he served so well by helping him steady his empire, ruled the greatest empire on earth for forty-one years—twenty-seven years B.C. and fourteen years A.D. Horace, however, a religious man, was loyal to his gods that preceded the Christian era. But, perhaps, Romans on the streets of Rome said nothing could ever happen to them. But as we know, two thousand years after Horace something did happen to that most powerful empire on earth.

From Roman Republic to Roman Empire, it fell in 476 A.D. at the age of 985 years. The ruins on three continents and numerous islands around the Mediterranean Sea tell part of the story of the greatness and grandeur, power and wealth that was once the Roman Empire. Latin tells the rest of the story. When and if you are in Rome, be sure to look up Palatine Hill where all the Roman emperors but Nero lived. You will see decadence on Palatine Hill, where once lived the powerful and the great. Now birds and bats have taken over the ruins of their palatial palaces, that little hill, the seat of power that once ruled the world. I have said in the beginning there are great similarities in our republic. I called it republic for I like the word, which some call us a democracy, which we are not. The right name for us is representative democracy. Do not forget we have a hill too, Capitol Hill, in Washington, D. C., a hill of power to all the world where thirty-six presidents, elected by votes and not bullets, have served.

Jesse and Naomi Deane Stuart at a party on the campus of the American University in Cairo, Autumn 1960.

FREEDOM WITHIN
FREEDOM'S WALLS

"What do you say we have a party for our classes?" Carl said.

"Wonderful," I agreed. "But where?"

"Oriental Room," he said.

"Reckon we could get that nice room?"

This was the place where guests from Egypt, America and other parts of the world are welcomed and given tea, coffee and pastries by our President, Deans and Heads of Departments. This was the nicest place to entertain at AUC.

"Yes, it will take a big room for your classes and mine," he said. "How about Thursday afternoon?"

"Wonderful with me. What can I do to help?"

"Sohair will handle all the details for me," he said. "We'll have coca colas, coffee and pastries!"

"I'm in for half the expense and you and Sohair plan it," I said.

"No, I have more students than you," he said.

"Not for me," I said. "I've never given such grades! But, I've never had such students. Best I ever had! Only one C and I could not give it. One C would have been lonesome alone so I lifted it to a B for a shy little Moslem girl! I love these Moslem students! They're out of this world!"

"I'm in for half the expense," I repeated. "You plan the party. Just so the students have a good time!"

"Yeah, they've worked hard," Old Carl said.

"Exams are over. We've had a lot of staying up all night studying and taking pills and fainting in class! It's all over now. Next fainting will be when the grades come in!" He laughed.

"I told you about 'em didn't I?" Carl said with a wink. All we have to do is put this affair in Sohair Mehhana's hands. She'll arrange everything, anything. She's a trusty, honest, reliable girl, and a bright one!"

"Eight A's and six B's in one class," I said. "Five geniuses in one class, two moslems and two Armenians and a Greek. Enough here to lift the future Literature of Egypt. I'm not giving them grades! They've worked for them! What else can they have?"

"A good time at a nice little school party. Now leave it to Sohair and to me!"

I left it to Old Carl. He loved his students more than teachers and more than people. To me he was the greatest teacher among us. And to his students he was all this and more. They loved him. Each got jealous of the one who would stand closer to him. If all Americans were loved half as much as Carl Leiden by half as many people who traveled or worked in countries of the world America would conquer the world through love.

Two days passed and I'd forgotten the party was on Thursday at 3 P.M. I was grading papers when the phone rang.

"Sir, you've forgotten the party." This was Sohair Mehanna's voice and she was just about our favorite student at AUC. "You must be here in a few minutes!"

"In five minutes," I said. "I'll grab a taxi! I'll

encourage one of these maddest taxi drivers in the world to drive faster."

"Don't kill yourself, Sir," she said. "Get here in one piece."

"Can I go, too, Daddy?" Jane asked. "Sounds great! I'm not in any of Dr. Leiden's or your classes!"

"You sure can," I said. "Come on! Let's go!"

We ran down the stairs.

"Allatax!" Our bowwab shouted as we went through the door.

The old man with the white handlebar mustache came.

"He'll get us there in two pieces!" I said to Jane as he pulled over to the curb. "Two pieces— you and me!"

We got in the taxi.

"Hurry," I said.

"All right."

He moved. We were there in three minutes by my watch. We went through the gate. We didn't take the elevator for one flight of stairs. When we reached the second corridor the noise poured out of Dr. Leiden's office. He had not been able to get the Oriental Hall. But who cared? If not the Oriental Hall why not Old Carl's office. It was the most popular room at AUC anyway. From here more tall tales, jokes, friendliness, and good laughter and happiness had generated than in any room at AUC. Maybe more good fun had generated here than in any one room in all Egypt! Jane and I headed straight for the laughter and the piano boogie-woogie! Old Carl got the piano from somewhere. We didn't ask where he got it. If the students wanted a piano he helped them.

The room was two-thirds jam-packed! How many students had gathered here I never knew! Students stood and sat in chairs and on the desks and the table! Old Carl was behind the piano in the corner grinning, his blue eyes laughing and his hands waving in the air. He was fenced in the corner with the piano—and big Mounir Boluos, a Coptic Christian who would make a couple fair sized men with pounds enough left over to make a boy, was making the piano dance! Smoke boiled up everywhere in the room.

In a University where a man's hands make enough happy noise on a piano to hold nearly a hundred students in a teacher's office, then these young people are hungry for something. This was a happy noise coming out of this office with the boogie-woogie and clouds of smoke.

"Dance," somebody shouted.

"Yes, dance."

"Yes, yes, yes."

This was something for quiet AUC, quiet and pious by American standards, but considered noisy as a jaybird among other schools in the Near East! We'd never asked authorities if this would be allowed! Just somehow we didn't think to ask.

"All right, who can Charleston?"

"Laila!"

"All right, Laila!"

A beautiful young woman stepped out. She was wearing black stockings, and long, black, pointed-toe slippers, a black skirt and a white blouse! And she could Charleston, too. She was Moslem, the daughter of a multi-millionaire. Her father had the lingerie shops and men's furnishing stores all over Egypt.

"Get in there with her, Jane," I said. "Charleston American style! You can do it!"

Jane stepped out into the little circle. Jane was much larger than Laila with more to move but she could about make the sparks fly from the floor! Amid the shouts and the laughter these two students, American and Egyptian, Christian and Moslem, set a fast pace. Now our noise was spreading. Dean Reid came first. He came and stuck his head in at the door. He might have cared about the smoke, for Latter Day Saints don't smoke. But they danced like mad! When Dean Reid saw the dancing, as fast as was ever put on by a couple of young women B. Y. (Brigham Young) in Provo, he grinned broadly and went away. The Charleston developed into a happy contest between these girls! But Laila outdistanced Jane. Jane was taller and larger but she had more weight to move, and the long black pointed toed slippers cracked longer on Old Carl Leiden's office floor than the American slippers!

When the girls were through Mounir Doss played a belly dance number, and Fadwa el Guindi, one of the most beautiful girls in Egypt, tall, slender, black Oriental eyes, and waves of black hair, a last year's graduate of AUC, stepped out on the floor. Fadwa El Guindi, now a star on one of Egypt's infant TV programs, was cheered madly. She, too, was Moslem, and a lovely of

121

lovelies, as graceful as a swan on placid waters! She was beautifully dressed like an Egyptian queen, rings on her fingers, bracelets on her arms, and ropes of multicolored beads around her neck. Her dance was beautiful. While she danced, Sameh Sika, an Egyptian Presbyterian, who had been involved in the fun episode by telling he had been beaten up at the Shagara and wearing patches on his face when nothing was wrong, stepped out and did the belly dance with lovely Fadwa. Sameh Sika is the best non-professional dancer in Cairo. When he watches the professionals dance he rises up. He can't sit still.

Just then our gentleman and scholarly dean, Dr. Namani, a very devout Moslem, came to the door where smoke, laughter and piano music issued forth in mixed swirls. Dean Namani smoked but the noise was too much. "I just wanted to see where the noise was coming from," he said.

"In here," Old Carl said.

He stuck his head over the piano and grinned at Dean Namani while Fadwa and Sameh continued their belly dance. Dean Namani knew Fadwa El Guindi and Sameh Sika and the dance was from his part of the world! He was familiar with this music and dance. He smiled and went back up the corridor to his office.

"President McLain will be here next," someone shouted.

When the belly dance was ended someone shouted: "On with the dance!"

Then Kimon Valaskakis stepped out on the floor. He was a tall, bearded Greek wearing his tight-fitting pants and long, black pointed-toed shoes. He was joined by his American partner, Jeannie Knorr. They were joined by fun-loving Sameh Sika, who had just finished a dance. Sameh was thin as a rail, all legs and arms and motion. His partner was plump Marianthi Coroneou, who was Greek and one of my A students, and Robert Tembeck, Armenian, the young genius on the stage, director of plays, creator of plays, poems, short stories and articles, and his partner was Marie Nagirski, Polish from America whose father was publicity director of United States Information Services. Mounir Boulos began the tune of the Greek folk dance, Hassapekos. Where had these youth learned to dance? Plump Marianthi Coroneou surprised everybody! But the Greeks in Egypt have never lost their heritage—not their folk dances! This was a fast and beautiful dance! Kimon's long feet tapped positively on the concrete floor to the music while he lifted his little Jeannie shoulder high in his swings.

Here was the Armenian, Greek, Polish, German, American, and Egyptian, the Roman Catholic, the Greek Orthodox, the Armenian Orthodox, the Egyptian Presbyterian dancing together. Here was the meeting of youth from four continents and five countries! Here were youth of the world having freedom and fun— loving their freedom and fun. Here were four of the students, Kimon, Marianthi, Jeannie and Robert, whom I had given A's in creative writing! What wonderful youth! In this room were students from 28 countries, who spoke 19 languages and 30 odd dialects.

The crowd cheered and the room got a little wild! Old Carl kept behind the piano grinning and waving his arms and enjoying the fun! Little Sohair Mehanna, one of Carl's former students, a devout Moslem and one we had never known to dance, went over and asked her teacher to dance with her. But Old Carl couldn't dance! That was why he was behind the piano.

Next was an American folk dance. "Where is your accordion, Robert?" a student shouted.

"I don't know," he said. "I don't need it anyway. I want to dance. And Mounir is making the piano do it all anyway!"

We thought he would beat the piano down, that it would fall apart, but the folk dance was on! And then another slower folk dance which I joined and danced with the students while teachers came running down the corridor to see where the noise was made. They gathered, watched us a few minutes and then moved on! When a teacher joined the students everything was all right!

Then they danced the Arab folk dance, Egyptian folk dances, but the last dance was a good finish. Kimon Valaskakis, Jeannie Knorr, Robert Tembeck, Laila Chourbagui, Daisy Kroub, Sameh Sika, Jane Stuart, and Faisall Farra showed them how to do an American dance, American style, the Rock and Roll. This was the dance they loved and one which brought the greatest applause. This was the last dance, for someone whispered President McLain was coming. We scattered in all directions. We had had fun and freedom within freedom's walls inside The Gate. Carl Leiden's classes and mine had celebrated the ending of the first semester in a style the students loved.

124

AMERICA IS STILL THE DREAM!

Spending tonight in the Wilderness Road Motel, Harrogate, Tennessee, I am sitting in an easy chair on the porch looking down and over the Lincoln Memorial University campus and over LMU's former farming land where I worked when a student from 1926 to 1929. One hundred yards below me is a railroad switch where carloads of coal used to be switched until Lincoln Memorial students could unload them with coalforks into trucks to be hauled to the furnace rooms of our school dormitories. Many a time I helped unload a carload of coal on that switch. One of the men who helped me is today one of the outstanding Baptist ministers in the South, while another administers the USAID program in Addis Ababa, Ethiopia.

Just across the new four-lane highway is the farm where I helped cut and shuck corn grown by Lincoln Memorial students. I helped farm this corn. Before I left Lincoln Memorial this land was converted to pasture land, where my alma mater had a dairy herd which furnished milk and butter for Lincoln Memorial students. Now, this new four-lane highway has cut deeply into the slope of the hill and has taken part of the farm where we used to work.

The Wilderness Road Motel was built near the old, winding, crooked highway over which thousands of tourist cars passed in the 1920's on their way from Northern states to Florida. This was a U.S. highway. I have ridden over it many times. Now this old road is used to come to this motel, and by the three families living in homes nearby. The new road which displaced this old, crooked, mountain climbing road is across the valley. The new four-lane road runs parallel to it. I have seen three roads in this area in my day over which automobiles rolled from North to South and from the South to the North.

Less than a quarter of a mile to our right is Cumberland Gap and Cudjo's Cave, which furnished an ample supply of fresh water in the 1920's for Lincoln Memorial University. I worked with a crew of Lincoln Memorial's young huskies, who were earning all their expenses as I was, to dig a water-line, lay pipes, seal them, across stony limestone land from Cudjo's Cave, across a low mountain to the campus. This was one of the biggest projects ever undertaken by Lincoln Memorial students. All of this work was done by student labor. We knew water from this cave never needed ice to make it cold. When a coal-stoking furnace needed repairs at one of the three boys' dormitories and we didn't have hot water for showers, we took them in this ice-cold water which was quite a thrill. Sitting here I can see from Cudjo's Cave to Lincoln Memorial University's campus.

I entered Lincoln Memorial University on $29.30 and in my stay of three school years and two summers, I received $2.00 of help from home. I never received a scholarship. I went to school a half day, worked a half day besides extra work after each meal, drying the pots and pans. And on Sundays I did extra work in the dining room and kitchen and when something went wrong with the plumbing.

Now what disturbed me here as I looked at this broad four-lane highway across the campus, was that it had taken so much of the front campus. It had taken the deep grassy home down in front of Norton Hall, which was the girl's dormitory. Down in this grassy bowl, in a Tennessee Springtime and summer, after the evening meal, boys and girls were permitted to meet and talk, mingle freely together for a social hour.

Often we sat on the grass, talked and sang old ballads and modern songs of the day. One we often sang, was *My Blue Heaven.* Over half of the students could play stringed musical instruments, guitars, mandolins, and dulcimers— playing music and singing for an hour each evening was our recreation. There weren't many places for us to go, and these were miles away and we had no transportation. Young women wouldn't have been permitted to go unless they were chaperoned.

On this bowl there were many youth who talked love and marriage. I'd like to know how many Lincoln Memorial couples became engaged where this four-lane highway now runs across this campus! Boys outnumbered girls about three to one. All the girls were very popular and deeply respected. They were, for most part, from mountain areas and from small towns in Virginia, Kentucky, and Tennessee. They were mostly from poor families and had to work for a part or all of their school expenses. Some few came from middle-class families who could afford an automobile in the 1920's. Young men and women came because they had ambitions to amount to something in the future.

In all my days at Lincoln Memorial I never heard sex acts discussed by the young men with whom I associated. As far as I know there were no "immoral acts" between women and men here from 1926 to 1929. And many of the women were feminine ladies, and the men were rugged and masculine. We had a select group of ambitious young people who came to Lincoln Memorial to prepare for life. They were willing to work, to go through hardships to attain their ambitions. More than a 100 names came back to me.

Today these youth hold some of the finest positions in America. Perhaps 175 books have been written by LMU writers and published by reputable houses. Newspapers and magazines have been edited by them. LMU's pre-med students who went on to become doctors are among the best. Today a number have built and operate hospitals in areas where there were no hospitals when they graduated. They've become fine lawyers, teachers, and diplomats to foreign countries. They've become outstanding ministers. What valuable citizens they have made for their native states and for our country! The old saying used to be: "If a LMU graduate can't do it, it can't be done!" There were forty applicants for one important position. One was a Lincoln Memorial graduate. He was chosen from the forty.

But over where the four-lane highway goes, something happened only a few will ever remember. The big elm stood there where Freshmen and upper classmen once had a royal battle in an intramural sports clash. I was one of the upper classmen in this battle. A white flag was tied in the top of the elm. We, the upper classmen, were to protect the flag in the tree and the lower classmen (Freshmen) were to take it down; we were permitted twenty huskies to preserve our flag, and they were permitted thirty of their younger huskies to take it down. We put eight of our men, good climbers, up in the tree.

On the ground the battle raged; twelve of us were battling thirty of them. We managed to keep them away from the tree for a while but we scarcely had enough clothes left on our bodies to hide our nakedness. When I looked over at my high school classmate, who was my roommate at LMU, Elmer Heaberlin, who was an upper classman and completely exhausted, he was lying on the grass in his shoes and underpants. Two were sitting on him, lower classmen, resting so they could do battle again. I tried to reach "Heab" to rescue him but I was too exhausted. Then I was pushed over and two rested on me. Now they were scaling the tree. They were pushed down by the feet of our upperclassmen. Many tumbled down to the grass. But they found a way to bring our men out of the tree. They hauled our flag down.

But down on the ground were men exhausted, bruised, and hurt. Several were taken to the hospital over the mountain in Middlesboro, Kentucky. This was a battle royal in Intramural Sports I would never forget. Never was another flag put up in a tree for men to protect and others to take down. In later years, I wrote a short story, "How Sportsmanship Came to Carver College" about this event which was published in *Esquire Magazine*. The elm was allowed to stand after its branches had been stripped. New branches grew again. Years later LMU students sat again under its shade down in this grassy bowl. But now when cars zoom over at high speeds, who will ever know or remember what went on beneath this road over which passengers ride?

In the afternoon we took a leisurely drive over the Lincoln Memorial University Campus. We had our difficulties getting across these new four-lanes; there was so much traffic in the tourist season over this main highway artery going North and South. So many of the old buildings were gone, including the old wooden-frame post office where our teacher of creative writing, Harry Harrison Kroll, used to post his short story and book manuscripts. When I was in the post office on evenings about the same time he was, for I carried student mail to the dormitories, Mr. Kroll would be there getting his mail. If he got a check for a short story anyone could see the joy written on his face. He smiled, shook his head, then tightened his lips. When he got rejections, as he often did, there was a puzzled look and a frown on his face. The corners of his lips seem to drop until his mouth was like a half moon with the bow up! Earlier we drove up to his little house to have a look. This was known as the Kroll House. He wrote his first novels here and many stories and poems. He also did his illustrations here for his poems, stories, and novels.

Then we drove down to see the trees the Smith Brothers and I set in front of the library. They had grown quite tall. I also had a look at the broad-topped eucalyptus tree under which my literary friends and I used to hold our meetings and where we came to write. A rival literary group held their meetings under another eucalyptus tree not too far away. This tree had died. Ours was still green and growing. But who now would remember what had gone on under those trees? Who would remember those who later wrote stories and poems that appeared in the *Atlantic Monthly, Harpers, Yale Review, Colliers, Saturday Evening Post, Esquire*? Our teacher, Harry H. Kroll wrote some of them too, but not nearly so many as his students.

Two new dormitories had been built since Naomi Deane and I were last here. One was erected on the University garden where we used to grow vegetables for our dining room tables. Another dormitory had been built on the edge of our cornfield where we grew corn to feed livestock on the University farm. Now all of this—dairy herd, gardening, and farming—had been discontinued. One youth who used to sleep

131

near the dairy barn so he could arise early to help milk the cows (this was in the days before milkers) was Ross Carter who wrote the fine book in World War II, *Those Devils in Baggy Pants.* He was a paratrooper. I thought of Ross Carter when we looked down at the large barn that would never be active again. And Ross Carter would never be active again.

Now the fields where we used to grow corn for our silo and for our bins looked weedy and wretched. The "chickery" which we called the building where we raised our chickens and got our eggs had fallen into decay. I worked only one Saturday at the "chickery." I remember this well for I worked with Paul Dykes, a student who would take a chew of tobacco. I got extremely hungry before quitting time and he told me to hold tobacco in my mouth and it would stave off hunger. I had never used tobacco then. I took a chew from his pouch which made me about as sick as I have ever been. This staved off hunger. I couldn't eat a bite until next morning.

We drove around the rainbow road up to Grant-Lee Hall. It was here I lived the three school years and two summers at Lincoln Memorial University. I had worked all over this dormitory cleaning and doing repairs. Ben Webb, who was driving the car, parked and I showed him, Naomi Deane, and Jean my old room from the outside. Up in my room I had written hundreds of poems, themes that later turned out to be short stories which were published in good magazines and in my story collections. Up in that building I had read a few hundred books, studied textbooks. I had taken ice cold showers too. In that room I had had my youthful dreams. This old dormitory, built by the English for a health resort, was like a home to me. Right now I have the picture of Grant-Lee Hall on one side of a small card-calendar which I carry in my billfold. I carried it around the world with me.

Lincoln Memorial University didn't look as sharp to me as it did in the days when I was a student here. Today at Lincoln Memorial University students don't have to work for all or any part of their expenses. This campus is minus that excellent student labor they had back in the 1920's and up until World War II. And the lack of this excellent labor, which has been replaced by hired help, is showing now. There is no comparison. Because we students came here then for the only chance in life we could get, because Lincoln Memorial University took us in when we had nowhere else to go, this school became our second mother. We loved, cared for, and protected Lincoln Memorial. We would have fought with our fists or with weapons for our school. It was our second mother, our home, our everything. For us this school stood between the darkness of ignorance and the light of our dreams!

As we drove away, I looked over the vast campus again. There wasn't any place I hadn't pushed a big lawnmower. Over the farm fields I had helped cultivate and harvest the corn. I had never milked cows but I could have milked them. I had helped build the faculty apartments. I had handled every brick that had gone into this building. There was scarcely a building (old ones) or a foot of ground on this vast campus and farm where I hadn't worked. I had not merely returned to see my alma mater but I had come back home. I felt that I owned a big part of Lincoln Memorial. Of course I had received small wages for my work. But I had comparable expenses. With $300 in cash a student could about pay his way for nine months at Lincoln Memorial from 1926 to 1929.

As to grades, I made a 2.2 standing out of a possible 3. I bought my own clothes (what I had) and books. My mother did the laundering of my shirts. I sent them to her 300 miles away. She always returned them in a paper box that glass jars came in that she used for canning. In an emergency I laundered and ironed my shirts. I pressed my extra suit. I kept only one suit with extra trousers. I went to Lincoln Memorial from the steel mills without a suit of clothes. I went there in a pair of Navy blue sailor pants with buttons across the front that my blue coat came down far enough to hide. This was my Sunday suit. I shaved with a long black-handled razor my father had given me. I left Lincoln Memorial owing one debt, this was to the school, $100.50, which I paid shortly afterwards from a $100 per month teaching check after $25.00 was subtracted each month for room and board.

To me, with more years behind than in front of me, America is still the dream. After so much travel, so many books, stories and poems, so many acres, stocks, cash—more possessions than we need—where else could a coal miner's son, a coal miner who couldn't read and write, in what other country could I have done better? In what other country (I have been in more than 90) could I have ever found another Lincoln Memorial University that would have given me an equal chance? America has given me the chance. At Lincoln Memorial I found the dream! But the chance comes to no one who does not go to seek and find.

ACKNOWLEDGEMENTS

"America is Still the Dream!", "The Importance of Reading in the Life of Man," "The Little Pencil Reminder on My Desk," and "Poverty of the Mind" first appeared in *Educational Forum* and are reprinted by permission of Kappa Delta Pi, An Honor Society in Education, owners of the copyright.

"The Professor Who Didn't Like Me," "The One-Room School Was Accelerated Too," and "Time and a Place for Growing Up" are reprinted with the permission of *The Peabody Reflector* where they first appeared.

"If I were Seventeen Again" first appeared in *Mountain Life & Work* and is reprinted with their permission.

"Character and the American Youth" first appeared in *The Baylor Line* and is reprinted with their permission.

"Guidance with a Heart" first appeared in *Education Summary* and is reprinted with the permission of Arthur C. Croft Publications.

"Stabilizing a Generation" first appeared in *Scimitar and Song* and is reprinted with permission.

"Memory Albums" first appeared in *The Tennessee Teacher* and is reprinted with permission of the Tennessee Education Association.

"What America Means to Me" first appeared in *A World of American Literature* and is reprinted with permission of American Book Company.

"Freedom within Freedom's Walls" first appeared in the *East West Journal*.

"My Seven Seven Year Plans" first appeared in *Phi Kappa Phi Journal*.

The photographs used throughout this book are from the Jesse Stuart family album.

Great care has been taken to find the owners of copyrighted materials and to make due acknowledgement. We will gladly rectify any omissions in future editions.